# The French Army of the Orient 1798–1801

## Napoleon's Beloved 'Egyptians'

Yves Martin

Helion & Company Limited

Helion & Company Limited
26 Willow Road
Solihull
West Midlands
B91 1UE
England
Tel. 0121 705 3393
Fax 0121 711 4075
Email: info@helion.co.uk
Website: www.helion.co.uk
Twitter: @helionbooks
Visit our blog at http://blog.helion.co.uk/

Published by Helion & Company 2017
Designed and typeset by Farr Out Publications, Wokingham, Berkshire
Cover designed by Paul Hewitt, Battlefield Design (www.battlefield-design.co.uk)
Printed by Henry Ling Limited, Dorchester, Dorset

Text © Yves Martin 2017
Images by the author or from the author's collection, © Yves Martin

Cover: 'Dromedary and Dromedary Trumpeter on Campaign'
watercolour by Eugene Leliepvre, © Yves Martin

Every reasonable effort has been made to trace copyright holders and to obtain their permission for the use of copyright material. The author and publisher apologise for any errors or omissions in this work, and would be grateful if notified of any corrections that should be incorporated in future reprints or editions of this book.

ISBN 978-1-911512-71-4

British Library Cataloguing-in-Publication Data.
A catalogue record for this book is available from the British Library.

All rights reserved. No part of this publication may be reproduced, stored in a retrieval system, or transmitted, in any form, or by any means, electronic, mechanical, photocopying, recording or otherwise, without the express written consent of Helion & Company Limited.

For details of other military history titles published by Helion & Company Limited, contact the above address, or visit our website: http://www.helion.co.uk

We always welcome receiving book proposals from prospective authors.

# Contents

| | | |
|---|---|---|
| Acknowledgments | | iv |
| Introduction | | vi |
| 1 | The French Expedition to Egypt 1798–1801: An Overview | 10 |
| 2 | The Men and their Daily Life | 23 |
| 3 | Doing Much with Little: Organisation and Tactics | 41 |
| 4 | Lining up the Troops: Orders of Battle of the Army of the Orient 1798-1802 | 73 |
| 5 | Uniforms – 'The Most Beautiful Sight the Eye Could Behold' | 103 |
| 6 | Conclusion, Sources, and Further Reading | 124 |

# Acknowledgments

As always, such a historical and technical work can only be achieved with the help of many.

The author must first and foremost thank the unsung heroes of the Service Historique de la Défense (SHD; the French war archives). For the last twenty-odd years, I have been there on many occasions. I have always found the staff to be diligent and helpful. Located in the Vincennes castle, going there is also an experience in itself. Vincennes was the home depot of the Imperial Guard artillery, then later the training ground for the first true chasseurs units in the 19th century. Ever since the reading room has moved to the renovated Louis XIV pavilion, readers go through the archive boxes in a magnificent room decorated with huge paintings showing the Sun King's battles, not to mention that one is welcomed in the entrance staircase by massive paintings by Detaille. All of this is to say that I have, and will continue to owe, a massive debt to the SHD as all good researchers do.

Second, my deepest gratitude to my editor, Andrew Bamford. Although I write and speak English since my childhood, this is my very first book in what I consider my second native language. It has been a lot of fun, and Andrew has really made it all the better.

Friends who are also enthusiasts of the period were also instrumental in my research. The 'Le Briquet' association in Orleans (founded amongst others by Jacques Brouillet, also a major researcher on Egypt) got me into this more seriously than ever before and taught me the fundamentals of uniformology as a branch of historical science.

My dear and close friend Vincent Bourgeot has been discussing with me all matters related to the Army of the Orient. His expert knowledge on period uniforms, equipment, weapons has few equals. He is always available to debate the tough questions I may have and help reach a conclusion or some consensus.

Likewise Alfred Umhey and Hans-Karl Weiss who have been both instrumental when the cloth samples were first found in the SHD archives. They have, willingly or not, pushed me even further into this research and they know it's still not concluded yet!

Jean-Yves Forthoffer, son of the truly great uniformology expert, Roger Forthoffer was kind enough to share his father's files on Egypt, which really helped adding a few missing pieces to this massive puzzle.

Arnaud de Gouvion Saint-Cyr, whose ancestor was not in Egypt, did however prove very worthy of his name by pointing out to me the never-seen-before period watercolours when they surfaced on the market. He is not only a true friend, but also an expert in the militaria field and it remains an honour and pleasure to exchange with him.

There are so many other friends with whom I have had casual or formal interactions around the topic of Egypt that I cannot list them all. I pray they forgive me for not putting their name down.

Finally, my deepest gratitude and love to my family who has to bear with my passion. Books, manuscripts, and plates have invaded our abode for years now. I have vanished off to Vincennes on many a Saturday, even more now as our sons have become independent adults. Yet their own patience, and my wonderful wife Magda's, has known no limit. Though they do not share my interest, they understand what it means to me, for this and all the love we share, I thank them.

# Introduction

The author of this book is a very lucky man. For him, Christmas can easily be a day of his choosing whenever in the year. His Christmas tree takes the form of a large, beautiful medieval fortress east of Paris, easily reachable by the metropolitan subway. His presents take the form of large black boxes attached with canvas strings. Like all good Christmas presents, what is in the box is unknown, and a surprise. It can be a wonderful, or disappointing. The fortress is the castle of Vincennes, home to the French war archives, and the boxes, the B6 series of these archives, devoted to the French Army of the Orient 1798-1801. There is no lack of such presents, as just the daily correspondence is represented by over eighty boxes, while other references hold senior officer correspondence registers, reports, troop returns, and so forth. For some twenty years now, the author has waded on and off through these papers: at times, digging at Vincennes into other topics, such as the campaign of 1815 or the Imperial Guard, but always coming back with eagerness and enthusiasm to the B6 series.

It all started in the early 1970s when my eyes came across the late Albert Rigondaud's (Rigo) remarkable very first article on the dromedaries in the new and catchy magazine "Uniformes". Over the next few years, Rigo would come back to what he called 'the extraordinary dress of the army of the Orient', and if the dromedaries had attracted my attention, the multi-coloured infantry uniforms were a shock. I read all I could on the topic and systematically came back to it. Why did a French army adopt a dress so odd and so against any of its traditions and which was never to be seen again? While visiting the rooms of the Musée de l'Armée in Paris, I also saw Rousselot's incredible watercolours representing the Army of the Orient. Again, I was awestruck by the variety and also by the fact it seemed to have been all but forgotten until some research came to be done in the late 19th and early 20th centuries.

For long, I thought all had been found and that Rousselot, Rigo, and others which I were to discover over time like Boisselier and Domange, had put the final nails in the coffin. We knew all what could be said about the Army of the Orient. And, having a scientific background, a life with a good job and family, I laid the topic to rest.

And then, chance made me meet up with other passionate hobbyists who like me had been or were figure modellers, but also researchers on the complex topic of uniformology. Through them I learnt of the importance of

# RÉPUBLIQUE FRANÇAISE.

LIBERTÉ.      ÉGALITÉ.

*Au Quartier – général du CAIRE, le 6 Brumaire, an 7 de la République française.*

ORDRE DU JOUR, du 6 Brumaire, an 7.

QUELQUES Français ont été tués le jour de la rébellion, et ces hommes sont du nombre de ceux qui n'exécutent pas les ordres qui ont été donnés, et qui ont l'imprudence de s'écarter de leurs quartiers, seuls et sans armes. C'est aux chefs des corps, aux chefs des administrations à veiller à ce que, hors du service, les Français ne s'exposent pas et sur-tout sans armes. Le plus grand ordre, la plus grande discipline doivent être maintenus parmi les troupes. Tout Français doit être bien armé, avoir ses armes en état et les munitions nécessaires. En cas de mouvement dans la ville, chacun doit se rendre à son corps; ou se réunir à son administration pour attendre les ordres qui peuvent leur être envoyés suivant les circonstances.

C'est dans le moment où la tranquillité règne, qu'on doit avoir la sagesse de ne pas se livrer à trop de sécurité, de se tenir toujours sur ses gardes, et de porter ses armes.

LE GÉNÉRAL EN CHEF est instruit que plusieurs soldats se permettent de s'insinuer dans les maisons, et y pillent. Il est ordonné au commandant de la place et aux chefs des corps, de prendre des mesures, telles que le soldat se tiennent dans les bornes de ses devoirs, et que quelque mauvais sujet, ne compromettent pas leurs camarades, et la tranquillité publique.

LE GENERAL EN CHEF ordonne, que le magasin-général fournira à la 69ᵉ. demi-brigade de quoi faire 1800 pantalons.

*Signé, Alexandre BERTHIER, Général de Division, Chef de l'État-major-général.*

*Pour copie conforme au registre d'ordres, l'Adjudant-Général, sous-chef de l'État-major.*

Original daily order published in Cairo on 27 October 1798. Composed of one or several pages depending on what had to be communicated to the troops, the Army of Orient daily orders are a major source on its actual daily life. Signed by the army's chief of staff (in this case Berthier), it was to be read aloud to all troops. One will note the specific Army of Orient symbol which combines the usual crown of laurels with a Phrygian cap (Revolutionary symbol of freedom) and two palm tree branches (symbol of Egypt).

always going back as much as possible to the original source, if at all possible a primary one.

This was around 1997-1998 and, since then, I've followed this advice and applied it in all the work I've done and published. It has proven an extraordinary and fulfilling exercise. I have learned that, as in many human endeavours, I know first and foremost what I do not know. I have come to be humble with whatever I found, challenging my conclusions and always questioning what may lie beyond.

This volume is an attempt at assembling much of what I found and gathered, especially in the B6 series of the French archives, but also through contemporary memoirs and the few iconographic evidence we have.

I will first state what it is not. This is not yet another book retelling the expedition in Egypt. This has been rather well taken care of, and in the concluding chapter, I give the reader suggestions for further reading if he so wishes. However, I cannot devote a book to the Army of the Orient bypassing any of its campaigns or pure chronological history: therefore the first chapter is a simplified timeline for the Army of the Orient and its campaigns.

This book also will make hardly any mention of the scientific aspect of the expedition. Indeed the scientific part of it had the most far-reaching consequences with the advent of Egyptology and the publication of the massive *Description de l'Egypte*, a publishing monument in itself requiring its own piece of furniture to house it! Again, this part has been widely documented and I feel there is little I can add.

My wish has been to write a book for those who have an interest in the deeper arcane of the military: organisation, orders of battle, dress and equipment. In many ways, the avid wargamer will, hopefully, find much of interest, but also the military historian looking for detailed facts.

The second chapter deals with the men and their daily life. The army was filled with colourful characters. If Bonaparte is well known to all readers, I am less certain for Kléber and especially Menou with the English-speaking public. Over the course of my research, I could not help admiring Kléber more and more for his leadership skills, his concise prose, and his pragmatism, and I took many lessons from him in my own daily life as a senior manager of individuals. On the contrary, Menou's flowery, long, and pompous prose, as well as his own inept management, showed exactly what not to do in terms of decision making and motivating teams! I hope that this chapter will bring the men of the Army of the Orient somewhat back to life to the reader and provide new anecdotes about them.

With the third chapter we get into 'the hard stuff'. This is all about organisation. I have tried as much as possible to dig down deep into unit set up and provide enthusiasts with detailed information. For this I have combined both the applicable regulations, but also the locally-made changes that one can read in the daily orders of the army. In a few instances, not all the information I would have wished to find has been found – especially for the more obscure local units. Hopefully, one day, those missing pieces will come to light.

The fourth chapter makes extensive use of the various boxes of the B6 series. This is probably the one part which will most appeal to wargamers. I have striven to come up with as many orders of battle as I could for all the important campaigning events the army went through. I have not, however transcribed all the material I have come across. I have had to make some choices due to some space limitation. The French Revolutionary and then Napoleonic armies were extremely well managed as regards administrative matters and returns. Napoleon was obsessed with data and is a model for any modern day business manager who thrives on facts to make decisions. This was also very true in Egypt. On campaign however, returns could be sketchy and papers lost. Therefore the Syrian campaign portion of this chapter may disappoint some – again, maybe somewhere a stack of papers will turn up from some forgotten private archives. Special mention must be made of an incredible return drafted under Menou which is several meters long. I still wonder how it could be in all fairness be consulted except if laid out on a very large table. I had myself to pull a few tables together in Vincennes, attracting the attention of other attending readers!

The fifth chapter addresses dress and equipment, my core topic. I could have written a full volume on this, but have tried to focus much of my prose on what is truly new. In the course of my research, I have come across actual samples of cloth used and also genuine period iconography which both confirms and challenges conclusions made by the likes of Vanson, Rousselot, and Rigo. I do believe we know have an accurate view of what the men wore under Kleber and Menou and specifically as they faced the British in 1801. I had first expressed this in a two-part article in the defunct "Soldats Napoleoniens" magazine. The recent finding of contemporary depictions of infantry and dragoons in Egypt has formally confirmed my findings while adding some further elements. Again, despite all this progress, all is not known and we can only hope there will be more important findings in the years to come. We still lack a genuine infantry cap or even a coatee. The only true actual piece of uniform worn in Egypt is the complete dress of a dromedary trumpeter housed in the Musée de l'Armée. A dromedary sabre also came up for sale recently, but outside of these pieces, and maybe one early cap in a private French collection, no other item is known.

Finally, there can be no real conclusion to such a book based on continuous research, and the concluding chapter is an invitation to readers to dig into the various existing works and, possibly, like me, into the marvels of archives whether in Vincennes or in other places I have had yet to dig into.

And to end as all letters of the period ended with a simple and apt wording

"Salut et fraternité"

Paris, Septidi, 17 Prairial, Year 225 (Monday, 5 June 2017)

# 1

# The French Expedition to Egypt 1798–1801: An Overview

**Origins of the Expedition**
On 27 July 1794, moderate members of the French Revolutionary government, then called the Convention, overthrew Robespierre's terror regime. They replaced it by the end of 1795 with the Year III Constitution, what became known as 'Le Directoire', the Directory. Its executive branch was composed of five directors. Every year, one director would be replaced. The new one would be appointed by the legislative chambers: the Council of Five-hundred and the Council of Ancients. The goal of such a design was to ensure that no one man would concentrate again all the power in his hand.

In effect, however, one man did to a large degree manage to do just that: Paul Barras. He had been the driving force behind the coup. His thirst for power was however largely a consequence of his taste for money and pleasure. Under him, money-making became the main occupation of the middle and upper classes of society. After the atrocities of the terror regime, the country was eager to renew with a life of leisure as it had enjoyed before 1789.

Although welcoming back many aristocrats who had survived the guillotine, the post-coup regime was still the French Republic and had no intent of restoring the monarchy. It was thus contested both on its left (the diehards of the Convention) and on its right (the monarchists who looked to the exiled Bourbon princes). This led to multiple insurrections in Paris in 1795 and 1796. In the fall of 1795, as the Directory was still being put in place, a group of royalists tried to seize power. On 6 October 1795, they were violently defeated by artillery and musket fire in front of Saint-Roch church in Paris. The government had turned for this to a young unknown general, Napoleon Bonaparte.

To thank him, the new Directory promoted him to général de division and gave him a minor command, that of the Army of Italy which was not expected to play any major role in the upcoming campaigns of 1796. On a more personal note, he had been introduced in Barras' close circle where he had met one of the politician's former mistresses, Joséphine de Beauharnais, whom he quickly married. Napoleon was on his road to glory and power. The campaign of 1796-1797 in Italy was, to everyone's surprise a decisive success. With military and political success on its side, the new regime was now firmly installed.

With Austria defeated and royalists almost totally crushed in the west, France had only one main enemy left, Britain. Bonaparte was named commander-in-chief of the Army of the Coasts of England. It soon became obvious that a direct and massive attack on England per se could not be successful. It was decided to strike England at its weakest points via a combined attack. In 1796, there had been a failed attempt due to bad weather at invading Ireland. This plan was yet again taken up in 1798 with the support of Wolfe Tone's Irish nationalists. Bonaparte had been sought to lead the force.

The Directory, however, and Barras especially, had become worried that Bonaparte's youthful glory could become a danger for them. Talleyrand, who had come back from emigration, had become foreign minister in 1797 and had come up with an ambitious plan to invade Egypt. The aim was to basically cut Britain's trade route with the orient, and especially India. The combined attacks were to choke England by striking at its main force, its economic wealth.

Bonaparte, as a typical 18th century nobleman, had been raised on the classics. The perspective of walking into the wake of conquerors like Alexander and Caesar was a decisive psychological boost. Although retaining nominally his title as commander of an army poised across the English coastline, on 13 February 1798, he had submitted a report on an invasion of Egypt to the Directory. On 5 March, he listed in detail the troops and means required to that end. On the same day, the Directory issued a number of decisions in support of it. The invasion of Egypt was now on its way with Bonaparte as its commander-in-chief.

Egypt was nominally under Ottoman rule. France and the Ottoman Empire had enjoyed a peaceful relationship since the days of King Francis I in the 16th century. This may seem odd for a country as strongly Catholic as France to have entertained for so long such close diplomatic ties, but this was the simple consequence of the old saying 'the enemy of my enemy is my friend'. The main continental enemy of France had been the Habsburg monarchy which was the Ottoman empire's main enemy too. Close commercial ties had been established between the southern French harbours, especially Marseilles. A system of trading establishments had been set up in the main cities of the Ottoman Empire. Known as the *échelles du Levant* (Scales of the Orient), these institutions represented France, but also Mediterranean Europe. Many French and Italian merchants from Marseilles and Genoa had branches all across the Ottoman Empire. One would also find French families having lived there for many generations, their scions practicing fluently both French and the various oriental languages. Individuals such as these would become 'dragomans', in effect indispensable interpreters and informal diplomats, key to trade and political relationships. For the most common business practice, a simple language had come to being, the 'sabir'. Formed from a combination of French, Italian, Turkish, and Arabic, with very limited words and a super-simplified grammar, it achieved its simple goal of ensuring adequate exchanges between merchants and sailors. The

# THE FRENCH ARMY OF THE ORIENT 1798–1801

Bonaparte in 1798 by Dutertre. Dutertre was an accomplished artist who followed the expedition. He specialised in portraits. By all accounts he was incredibly gifted and his works truly conveyed the actual likeness of the individual. French public collections hold several of his original ink and watercolour works. A large series of portraits from Egypt were published as such, but a slightly small selection was included in the Histoire *Scientifique et Militaire de l'Expédition d'Égypte*. The portraits featured in this book come from this published source.

importance of these Franco-Italians must not be underestimated. Without them, the army would not have been able to withstand three years of occupation, so far away from France and with its supplies line almost completely cut. Genoese merchants like the Pini Brothers had offices in Marseilles, Genoa, Alexandria, and Cairo, and as we shall see they were instrumental in equipping and clothing the Army of the Orient.

Egypt, like the rest of Ottoman North Africa, was somewhat on the side-lines of all this. The real ruler of Egypt was not the Ottoman Empire, but the Mameluke class. Mamelukes had been instituted in the middle-ages by the Turks as a warrior class raised from captured Georgians and Circassians. Converted to Islam, Mamelukes were therefore not Egyptian natives, but due to their strength had gradually become the true rulers of the country, although the Ottoman Empire still had representatives and was still levying taxes there.

France, being the ally of the Ottoman Empire could justify its invasion of Egypt by proclaiming it was there to help the Empire restore its true rule over the country. This, at least, was the excuse which would be given to the population and to the rest of Europe. But no-one would be fooled, all knew that in the end, the aim was to expand the power of France to the expense of Britain's influence leveraging the increasing weakness of the Ottomans. What became to be known as 'the great game' was about to begin.

Bonaparte's recent successes had attracted some of the Revolution's most brilliant officers. Amongst them Kléber, who had been in semi-retirement, and Desaix, who had been so impressed by Bonaparte's victories that he had travelled to Italy to visit each of the recent battlefields to better understand them.

In less than three months, Bonaparte and his staff assembled some 38,000 men and over 300 ships. In addition to these men, a number of servants and women have to be added. Servants were officially welcome, but not necessarily listed on ship returns. Women had been very limited in numbers, but quite a few were smuggled on board. In total, the force amounted probably to 40,000 individuals. As a comparison, Rochambeau's troops sent to America less than twenty years before numbered less than 6,000 men!

From a strict military aspect, the expedition to Egypt stands out as an exceptional effort. Even more so, when one realises the conditions and constraints of the age of sail. Much has to be attributed to Bonaparte's iron will and the overall Revolutionary fervour and discipline. However, these very same qualities made him over-estimate the abilities of the French fleet. The pre-1789 French royal navy had some of the best vessels, officers, and crew in the world and had proven a match for the British during the American War of Independence. Unfortunately, many of the best officers were now gone. They had either emigrated or been killed during the Terror.

The expedition also included a little over 150 scientists and artists. This is nowadays the better known part of this adventure. Although there were westerners living in Egypt, the majority of their dealings were purely commercial. As a land, Egypt was as unknown then as parts of Amazonia or Antarctica are today. The scientific side of the invasion had without doubt some of the longest lasting and positive consequences ever of a military event. However, without some of these scientists, the army could not have survived, as we shall see.

## Timeline

19 May 1798: The various expeditionary fleets leave Marseilles, Toulon, Genoa, and Civita-Vecchia. The lead vessel is the *Orient*, on board of which is Bonaparte and his immediate staff.

10 June 1798: The expedition reaches Malta. The assault is given and in a day, the Knights of Malta surrender.

13-18 June 1798: Within six days, Bonaparte organises the new government in Malta. For the next three years Malta is under French Revolutionary rule. Bonaparte leaves an occupation force in the island under the command of General Vaubois. This body of troop is known as Division Vaubois. On the other hand, former Maltese troops are encouraged to join the expedition, forming the Maltese Legion. Some of the Knights of Malta of French extraction also join the force as officers.

1-2 July 1798: The expeditionary force lands near Alexandria and captures the town. There is little resistance and losses are relatively few although both Generals Kléber and Menou are wounded in the assault. Most of the French who had imagined Alexandria in its former ancient glory are shocked to discover its present-day reality. This is the first real contact with Egypt, its culture and its people.

14 July 1798: Battle of Chebreiss – this is the first clash with Mamelukes under the command of Murad-Bey

21 July 1798: At Embabeh, the French force enjoys a decisive victory over the Mameluke army. This battle fought under the shadows of the pyramids immediately receives the name of Battle of the Pyramids by Bonaparte. To defeat the Mamelukes, Bonaparte put the army in the usual square formations used against cavalry. However, the squares were much more massive with artillery posed at each angle, with cavalry and baggage trains at the centre. At no point could the Mameluke charges overcome the infantry walls which presented a combination of intense volley fire and cold steel.

Kléber in 1798 by Dutertre. We rarely have a profile view of Kléber, himself a gifted artist who did self-portraits.

Of the Mameluke leaders, Murad-Bey flees into Upper-Egypt, and Ibrahim-Bey towards Syria.

24 July 1798: Bonaparte and the French army enter Cairo. The French headquarters are placed on Ezbekieh Square in the house of Elfi-Bey. Bonaparte's immediate attention is to ensure a new government for Egypt. He issues a proclamation which states that Egypt has been freed from Mameluke tyranny and is to be brought back to full control of the Ottoman Empire. He sets up a 'Diwan', inviting prominent native Egyptians to join in the control and management of the country.

1-2 August 1798: the Battle of the Nile or of Aboukir Bay. The French fleet under the command of Admiral Brueys, whilst at anchor in Aboukir Bay, is surprised by Admiral Nelson's fleet. In a fight which starts at dusk and through the night, the French vessels are almost all sunk. This disaster culminates sometimes after midnight with the explosion of the admiral ship *Orient*. Brueys and most of the senior officers are killed. The French expeditionary force, deprived of its fleet, has now become the prisoner of its own conquest. Those sailors who have survived, either swimming back to the shore, or released after having been taken as prisoners by the British are organised into an infantry force called the Nautical Legion.

22 August 1798: Bonaparte creates the Institute of Egypt. In so doing he gives formal structure to the scientific branch of the expedition. The Institute will hold regular meetings for the next three years and issue a number of publications on all kinds of topics ranging from natural sciences to economy. Its greatest achievement is of course the birth of modern Egyptology. Following the return to France, all this work will be combined in a landmark massive publication *The Description of Egypt*.

26 August 1798: General Desaix departs with his division for Upper-Egypt in the pursuit of Murad-Bey and his men.

20 September 1798: First celebration in Cairo of the foundation of the French Republic. The French, wishing to impress the Egyptians, build a wooden obelisk in the centre of Ezbekyeh Square with inscribed on it the names of those who have fallen up to now. They also launch a balloon.

7 October 1798: In the Faiyum oasis area, Desaix achieves a victory over Murad-Bey at Sediman. Desaix has conquered the Fayum, but Murad-Bey flees further into Upper-Egypt as Desaix, having no cavalry, could not pursue him.

21 October 1798: The first insurrection of Cairo. The French are totally taken by surprise. Under the inspiration of religious leaders of the Al-Azhar Mosque, several thousands of inhabitants take to the street assaulting any French they can get their hands upon. General Dupuy, commander of the Cairo garrison, is killed. On the 22nd, Sulkowski, one of Bonaparte's most promising ADCs is slaughtered in the streets, quite literally hacked to pieces (his remains could only be identified thanks to what remained of his moustache!). The French bombard the city, especially Al-Azhar, and bring down the insurrection. The French have lost about 250 men, and the insurgents some 800. All men who have been captured weapon in hand are executed. Six El-Azhar sheiks who are detained are also killed, while nine others are condemned to death in their absence. Other parts

of the country remain agitated throughout the month of October. The French put a quick stop to any movement by violent reprisals. From now on, the French know that they will be able to stay in Egypt only as long as they establish a strong and constant military force. The Cairo rebellion has been neither inspired by the Mamelukes, nor really by the Ottomans, but by religious fanaticism. For the next three years, the French will have to face locally those three enemies, and not just the Mamelukes as they initially thought.

6 December 1798: Bonaparte sends a force of cavalry under General Davout in support of Desaix' division in Upper-Egypt. Aside from bringing much needed mounted troops to Desaix, this will be Davout's 'big break' as he will from now on follow Desaix and in turn be noticed by Bonaparte and become one of the future Napoleon's most trusted marshals.

16 December 1798: Now reinforced with cavalry, Desaix moves south in the pursuit of Murad-Bey. This campaign will lead him to the cataracts of the Nile. In addition to the military side of this expedition, the scientists and artists who are with Desaix will document the many discoveries they will make, more especially, Vivant-Denon, later founder of the Louvre museum.

24 December 1799: Bonaparte leads a small expedition to Suez and the Fountains of Moses. The group rides along the Red Sea and examines the ruins of the former canal. During this trip, Bonaparte is convinced of the usefulness of having troops mounted on dromedaries. Upon his return on 9 January 1799, he creates the Dromedaries Regiment, drawing its men from infantry units.

22 January 1799: Desaix catches up with Murad Bey at Samhoud and beats him. Once again, the French infantry proves itself against the Mameluke charges. Murad-Bey retires further, trying to preserve what is left of its demoralised forces. Desaix organises the occupation of the land he has secured. He spreads both his land troops and flotilla.

10 February 1799: With intelligence having reported that an Ottoman army is concentrating around Damascus, Bonaparte decides to move out with a large part of his army into Syria via Palestine and the Holy Land. This is the beginning of the Syrian campaign. His hope is also probably to break the deadlock that the Army of the Orient is in. By defeating the Turks, he hopes to open up a way back to France or on to British India.

11 February 1799: At Redecieh, Davout fights with his cavalry against the Mameluke forces of Osman-Bey. The French victory is far less decisive than usual with 37 killed and 44 wounded. This proves that the French cavalry still needs to be cautious against the Mamelukes. Sporadic fighting occurs across Upper Egypt as Arab reinforcements make their way from Mecca.

21 February 1799: The French army captures the outpost of El-Arisch after a protracted siege. This is the first indication that the campaign will not be as easy as the conquest of Egypt.

24 February 1799: Gaza is captured by the French forces.

1 March 1799: Capture of Ramleh.

# THE FRENCH ARMY OF THE ORIENT 1798–1801

3 March 1799: Desaix' flotilla is attacked by Osman-Bey and the Meccan troop just above Benut. All the boats are captured and the crews and passengers (sick and wounded mainly), slaughtered. The main boat *l'Italie* is set on fire by its commander before he dies. Desaix loses there most of his supplies and is obliged to ask for more to Bonaparte. On the same day, Desaix and his force reaches Aswan.

6-8 March 1799: General Belliard moves on to attack the village of Keneh where Osman-Bey's troops are entrenched. He has with him the 21st Light Demi-Brigade and elements of the 61st and 88th Line Demi-Brigades and of the 20th Dragoons. He is victorious and recaptures some of the boats, guns and supplies taken on 3 March. Enemy losses are estimated at 600 Meccans and 12 Mamelukes. On the French side, 35 dead and 134 wounded. Belliard reports that the Meccans made good use of the guns and ammunitions fighting house after house, forcing him to set fire to them to avoid more bloodshed on his side.

6-7 March 1799: Storming of Jaffa and massacre of the prisoners. The Ottoman garrison is promised to be spared, but is ultimately executed by shooting and bayonets on the seashore. Four thousand men die. This is the first element of Bonaparte's 'black legend'. In truth, Bonaparte had never thought of sparing the Turks as he knew he would not be able to support such a large body of prisoners on his way north.

9 March 1799: Plague has started out in Jaffa and Bonaparte visits the sick at the hospital.

13 March: In Europe, France declares war on Austria.

17-20 March 1799: The siege of Acre begins. Djezzar-Pacha, known as 'Djezzar the Butcher' reigns supreme of his city and most of the countryside. Taking Acre is the key to any further French progress. Bonaparte places much hope on his siege artillery which, given its weight, is travelling by boat from Egypt. Unfortunately it is captured by the British. In Acre, Djezzar is helped by Commodore Sydney Smith who also commands the British flotilla and by the engineer Phélippeaux. The latter was a former classmate of Bonaparte at the Royal Military School in Paris. Like him, he is an extremely gifted officer, but has emigrated. Ever since their schooldays, he and Bonaparte have been rivals. Phélippeaux persuades Djezzar to reinforce the walls of Acre. His and Smith's skilful advice and command of the besieged forces prove decisive during the entire siege. Phélippeaux dies just after the end of the siege in April 1799, either out of exhaustion or of the plague.

8 April 1799: A relief force is sent from Damascus to attack the French. Bonaparte dispatches Kléber's and Junot's troops. Junot resists against the enemy army at Nazareth on 8 April.

9 April 1799: Death of General Caffarelli during the siege of Acre. This is a major blow to Bonaparte as he was a supremely experienced officer in command of all engineers.

16 April 1799: Kléber catches up with the Turkish forces at Mount-Thabor. Conscious of the odds which are not in his favour, Bonaparte rushes to his help with two divisions. Combined, they crush decisively the relief army.

20 May 1799: Despite having received some siege artillery and successfully breached the walls at some point, Acre still has not fallen. The army has been decimated with the plague and there is little option but to turn back and retreat to Egypt.

27 May 1799: While stopping at Jaffa, Bonaparte visits again the sick. To this day, it is unknown if he actually gave the order to kill those who could not follow by poisoning to avoid them suffering painful death by the Turks.

14 June 1799: The French army makes a victorious entry into Cairo. Troops have been asked to place laurel wreaths around their headdresses. Bonaparte, although knowing the Syrian campaign is a defeat, cannot allow himself and the army to lose face in front of the Egyptians. This will be one of his first attempts at turning a defeat into a victory via propaganda. As a token of trust and gratefulness, Cheik El-Bekry presents Bonaparte with a young Mameluke servant, the soon-to-be-famous, Rustam-Razah, who will follow him up to the first abdication in 1814.

During the course of May and June, French armies in Europe are struggling against combined Austrian and Russian forces. The news reaches Egypt. Bonaparte understands that he is now too far from where the main events are happening and that he is unable to play any major role. He starts planning in secret to leave for France.

14 July 1799: A large Turkish army lands at Aboukir with the support of a combined Anglo-Turkish fleet. Their aim is clearly to take advantage of what seems to be a weakened French army.

24 July 1799: Bonaparte concentrates the army around Aboukir to throw back the Ottomans into the sea.

25 July 1799: Decisive victory of Aboukir. There is no longer a Turkish threat to Egypt. From the prisoners, Bonaparte recieves confirmation of the French defeats in Europe and this confirms him in his decision to leave.

28 July 1799: In Europe, all of Italy has fallen back into allied hands. The Italian sister republics have been abolished.

23 August 1799: Bonaparte with a few selected officers and men boards the frigate *Muiron* and sails for France. French scouting parties are surprised to find the horses of several general officers on the beach and report back to Kléber. Only Menou had been in the confidence. He hands out to Kléber a letter from Bonaparte explaining his decision and naming him commander-in-chief of the army.

Autumn of 1799: Kléber is much shocked by Bonaparte's departure. A hard-core republican, he sees in this almost a desertion in the face of the enemy. He writes a report on the state of affairs in Egypt back to the Directory. He insists that the best option is to secure a safe passage back for the army to France in order to bring these much needed troops back to help the republic. In his various letters he does not shy away from expressing his feelings about Bonaparte.

As commander-in-chief, his immediate attention is for the well-being of his troops. He very swiftly puts in place multiple orders to ensure that more revenue comes in as the financial situation of Egypt is quite dire. By the end of 1799 he has clothed and equipped the troops again. Overall the supply situation has improved thanks to his careful and forceful management. Kléber is beloved by his men, but also more feared and respected by the Egyptians than ever Bonaparte was. Given the poor communications with France, Kléber's letters and reports arrive after Bonaparte has seized power. The new regime will quietly ignore the tone of the letters and comments against the man who is now France's new strong man.

9 October 1799: Desaix finally crushes Murad-Bey near Sediman. Murad-Bey, defeated, accepts French rule and becomes their ally.

31 October 1799: Desaix is called back to Cairo by Kléber and sent to defeat a small Turkish force which has landed near Damiette.

9-10 November 1799: In France, the 'Coup of 18 Brumaire'. Bonaparte and some other conspirators overthrow the Directory regime. A new constitution is to be drafted

25 December 1799: In France the new Year VIII Constitution is put in place. The executive branch is now composed of three consuls, with the first (Bonaparte) having prominence over the others. This is the first step to supreme power for Bonaparte.

11 January 1800: Negotiations with the Turks start at El Arish under the leadership of Desaix and with the presence and advice of Commodore Sidney Smith.

28 January 1800: Kléber and the Ottomans along with Commodore Sidney Smith sign the Convention of El Arish. Under this agreement, the French Army of the Orient will leave Egypt within the next few months and be repatriated to France on board ships of the Royal Navy. In preparation for this, French troops start to evacuate their many outposts, concentrating on Cairo and Alexandria, while the Ottoman army approaches. By late February the Ottoman and French armies are in sight of each other in the Cairo area.

3 March 1800: Desaix leaves for France on board a merchant ship. With him are his aides, Savary and Rapp, but also his cavalry general, Davout. They are all confident that the recently signed convention will ensure safe passage for them. They area however captured by British forces off the coast of Hyères near Toulon and detained until 29 April 1800.

18 March 1800: The British government having refused to recognise the El Arish convention, the only option which is indicated to Kléber is that of an unconditional surrender. This being unacceptable Kléber issues a daily order to the army where the British reply is printed and at the end he states that 'to such insults, one can only reply with victories – soldiers prepare yourselves for the fight'.

20 March 1800: French forces under Kléber advance on to the Turks and thoroughly defeat them at Héliopolis. Yet again, French infantry discipline has prevailed. However, the Turks incite the inhabitants of Cairo to rebel again.

27 March – 22 April: Second Cairo rebellion. The French army sets siege in front of Cairo. Even more than with the first rebellion, the repression is fierce.

May 1800: Now with no hopes of immediate return to France, Kléber and the troops settle in.

# THE FRENCH EXPEDITION TO EGYPT 1798–1801: AN OVERVIEW

13 May 1800: Bonaparte and the Army of Reserve cross the Alps and fall on to the Austrian troops in Italy.

11 June 1800: Desaix and his staff finally join Bonaparte at his headquarter in Stradella. On 12 June, Desaix is sent out towards Novi to come to Suchet's help with two divisions.

14 June 1800: Decisive victory of Marengo over the Austrians. The outcome hung for long in the balance. Desaix, hearing the roar of the artillery, decides to come to the help of the main army and arrives towards the end of the afternoon. Charging at the head of a light infantry demi-brigade he is shot in the heart and dies immediately.

In Cairo while inspecting his residence and visiting his gardens, planning on improvements to be done, Kléber is stabbed to death by a fanatic from Aleppo. Both Bonaparte's main lieutenants in Egypt die on the same day, and almost at the same hour.

The French generals in Cairo assemble in the evening and discuss what to do next. They agree to follow strictly regulations and decide on having General Menou as commander-in-chief as he has been in the rank of général de division the longest. From a strict overall competence standpoint, the choice should have been in favour of Reynier, but he himself had opted to follow military law in this matter.

Summer and Autumn 1800: Menou, who has converted himself to Islam, is in favour of maintaining a French presence in Egypt and actually building a colony. His decisions typically alienate the Coptic community which has been quite instrumental in tax collection and other administrative matters.

Although an able, even talented, administrator and manager Menou does not have the confidence and love of the troops. His pompous and lengthy prose, as well as his well-known lack of any military talent, do not improve his standing over time. Worse, he gradually isolates himself from his generals, Reynier especially. At a time when he most needs support and cohesion within the army and especially his most direct subordinates, this will bring the downfall of French Egypt.

5 September 1800: Fall of Malta, captured by British forces. This will give a base for Britain to land in Egypt.

October 1800: The British plan to kick the French out of Egypt is decided. General Sir Ralph Abercromby's force will invade by sea with the support of the Turks, while a force assembled between India and the Cape of Good Hope under General Baird will drive inland from the Red Sea.

24 November 1800: British troops assemble in Malta

28 November 1800: Europe, General Moreau defeats the Austrians at Hohenlinden. This final and decisive victory forces Austria into asking for peace. The allied coalition is breaking down. Tsar Paul I comes into discussion with Bonaparte and agrees to close off trade with Britain. This puts pressure on Britain to achieve a victory in Egypt.

20 December 1800: Abercromby's force sails for Marmorice Bay near Rhodes, which will become a rallying and training point until they are ready to land in Egypt. General John Moore is sent to Jaffa to coordinate actions with the Ottoman Empire.

**22 February 1801:** The British forces leave from Marmorice Bay for Egypt.

**8 March 1801:** British troops led by General Moore land at Aboukir Bay. General Friant opposes them, but with insufficient strength and decisiveness. The British manage to establish a beachhead.

**12 March 1801:** In a quasi-repeat of the invasion of 1798, the British march on to Alexandria. Menou decides to go on the offensive and leaves Cairo with a body of troops, 6,000 strong. General Belliard is left in command of Cairo.

**13 March 1801:** British and French forces clash at Mandora. The French retreat into Alexandria.

**19 March 1801:** Menou arrives with reinforcements in Alexandria

**21 March 1801:** Battle of Alexandria (in French, Canope). The French attack before daylight. After a first initial success through a commando action by Dromedaries, the French infantry march to assault the British entrenched in the ancient ruins of Canope. Given the lack of visibility, some of the French columns loose themselves and the assault, far from being effective, turns into confusion. Menou, despite disagreement from his subordinates, decides to launch a massive cavalry charge into the British camp. General Roizé who leads the cavalry obeys although he knows this is a doomed attack. Roizé is killed and most of the French cavalry is crushed. Abercromby is fatally wounded during the attack and dies a few days after on board ship in Aboukir Bay. General Hely-Hutchinson is now in command. Menou locks himself up with what remains of his forces into Alexandria. The French are now split between Alexandria and Cairo with no means of regrouping their army.

**25 March 1801:** Turkish forces join the British. One force lands at Aboukir Bay, while another comes down from Syria.

**1 April 1801:** Baird's force sails from India. He lands at Kosseir in Upper-Egypt in May and is joined by the force coming from the Cape. Up through the month of June he will move up towards Cairo, but will arrive after the French surrender of the town.

**2 April 1801:** British capture Rosetta.

**13 April 1801:** The Alexandria garrison is fully cut off from any help following the flooding of Lake Mareotis.

**26 April 1801:** A British force is left with General Coote in front of Alexandria while General Hely-Hutchinson and the Turkish forces move on to Cairo.

**9 May 1801:** French defeat at Rahmaniyah. The last possibilities of communication between Alexandria and Cairo are now gone. Both forces are fully isolated while Ottoman forces are also moving in from the east.

**21 June 1801:** Start of the siege of Cairo by a combined British and Ottoman force.

**27 June 1801:** With no hopes of relief and a fully demoralised force, Belliard decides to surrender Cairo and his 13,000-man garrison.

**15 July 1801:** Belliard's force is brought to Rosetta. The agreement reached with the British is that they are to re-embark for France. They start to leave on 30 July 1801.

**9 August 1801:** All British and Turkish forces are now in front of Alexandria and the siege truly begins.

30 August 1801: After resisting almost a month, Menou finally gives in and surrenders. All French troops are now to leave Egypt, and embark on 14 September 1801. Despite having had the assurance all scientific material could be kept, it is confiscated by the British, including the famous Rosetta Stone. The French do manage to bring back all scientific notes and drawings.

1 October 1801: Peace of Amiens signed between Britain and France. This puts a temporary end to the conflict between France and the rest of Europe.

## Aftermath

The immediate consequences of the Egyptian expedition were many fold. Despite or maybe because of the ultimate French defeat, peace was signed between Britain and France offering some respite to both countries. The French military experience in Egypt was probably one of the driving forces behind several tactical and technological innovations which were put in effect during the Napoleonic Wars. The infantry scout formations, organised in 1799, seem very much like a prelude to the creation of the elite companies of voltigeurs in 1803. The 'Egypt square', although never fully formalised as part of the infantry manoeuvre regulations, could be found in most tactical manuals as an appendix. The small arms system of Year IX, actually an evolution of the 1777 system, incorporated a short cavalry musket which had been first designed and widely distributed in Egypt also to infantry officers, sappers, and drummers.

On the human side, officers and men who had survived Egypt were for the greater part cherished by Bonaparte. Although Menou was given a rather obscure desk job, he was never publicly disavowed. Davout, Bertrand, Desgenettes, Larrey, Daure and others. all had a distinguished career under the Empire, and this can be also said of lower ranks. Native troops who had been pressed into the French infantry, or who had joined in the more exotic corps like the Coptic, Greek, and Syrian Legions continued to fight for France. The Mameluke squadron which became part of the Imperial Guard in 1802 joining the old Guides is the most well-known example. However, there was also the Chasseurs d'Orient, one of those 'special' legions composed of non-French soldiers, in this case men coming from the eastern Mediterranean, and, more plainly, many Egyptians or men from Darfur continued their career in French ranks.

In the longer run, consequences were even more massive. Malta was now in British hands and was to remain until its own independence. Egypt had had a taste of true independence from the Ottomans through the incursion of the French and the British. This was to lead to modern Egypt and its own independence during the 19th century. Obviously the birth of modern Egyptology and continued strong ties between France and Egypt in that aspect remain to this day.

But there was another, lesser-known consequence. As the French army needed supply it went to various French-Italian merchants active in the wider Mediterranean area. Some of them found sources in the western part of the Ottoman Empire, what was then known as the Barbary Coast, the regencies of Algiers and Tunis. One of these ill-concluded commercial deals some thirty years later led to a conflict between Algiers and France providing the justification for yet another invasion. In the conquest of Algeria, the French army turned back to the experiences of Egypt, to the point that one of the official interpreters who negotiated the surrender of the Bey of Algiers had been with the Army of the Orient in 1798.

# 2

# The Men and their Daily Life

**The Generals and Staff**
Who were these men who sailed out of southern France and Italy to conquer Egypt? For the most part, they were young by our current standards. This was especially true of the senior leadership. Out of the thirty-one generals, eleven were less than thirty and only five over fifty, and nine between forty and fifty!

This youthfulness did not always extend down to the lower officer ranks. Senior regimental ranks of brigade commander or battalion/squadron commander were for the most part in between thirty and fifty, which pretty much corresponds to what one can observe later on during the imperial period. The junior commissioned ranks, up to and including captain, were however massively occupied by men of that very same age group with a strong share of them being in the upper bracket. Worse, if only eight senior regimental officers were above fifty, that number rose to around fifty for the junior officer ranks.

The contrast between the youth of the generalship and the seniority of the more junior officers seems like a complete contradiction, but can easily be explained. As it left for Egypt, the army had about 2,500 officers of all ranks. Of these, only a minority had served in the royal army before the start of the war in April 1792. The most striking statistic is that only 87 (3.5 per cent) had then held a commission as officers. 295 (12 per cent) were NCOs and 717 (29 per cent) simple rank and file. In total this means that only 44.5 per cent of the officers had been in the army before 1792. The rest had come from the volunteer battalions raised to defend the homeland. These Volunteers of Year II, as they came to be known, came from all walks of life: some had had previous military experience, but on the whole, they were new to the army. It did present a major opportunity for many: six of the Army of the Oreint's generals came from this background, two of whom – Lannes and Murat – had joined as simple volunteers and risen through the ranks. The greater part of the former royal army NCOs and soldiers were typically fairly senior individuals for the time, above thirty and quite frequently above forty. Although undoubtedly gifted for the military profession, the monarchy had not allowed them to rise above the ranks they held before 1792. At best they could have hoped to become first lieutenant in their regiment and then retire.

The Revolutionary army provided a major opportunity for these men and allowed quite often a meteoric rise provided that they survived the early battles. Not only was their experience a real asset, but, furthermore, many of the royal officers had left the army to join the counter-revolutionary forces either in the émigré corps abroad or in the west. The consolidation of volunteer forces with the regular army reinforced the need for experienced leaders and this explains the structure of the leadership of the army in Egypt.

Another key global aspect to consider is that almost all of the units that composed the army had fought before with Bonaparte in Italy. Obviously the commander-in-chief was used to these troops and trusted them; also the men were coming for the most part from southern France or Italy and it was expected that logically they should cope better with the hot Egyptian climate.

Before looking into the plain regular soldier, it is worth diving somewhat into the details of the leadership. Out of the 35,000 men who left for Egypt in 1798, close to a thousand composed the headquarters and administration, and a little under two hundred more were scientists & artists. As stated, thirty-one generals provided the top military leadership, but no one had foreseen that the war commissary and medical services, as well as some of the scientists and intellectuals, would play as important a role as the general officers in the achievements and survival of the expeditionary force.

The army over the course of the three years was led by three successive commanders-in-chief. Each was quite different in character, style and skills and it is worth spending some time looking into these contrasting individuals.

Napoleon Bonaparte was, even by French Revolutionary standards a very young general. As he sailed out for Egypt, he was only twenty-nine years old. Born into minor Corsican nobility, the Revolution provided him with opportunities he could never have had under the monarchy. He had surprised everyone with a string of amazing victories in Italy. He displayed there a military talent unseen up to now within the French military leadership. He also not only defeated Austria and its Italian allies, but actually set up 'sister republics', effectively satellite states of revolutionary France. In so doing, he acquired a taste for political power and received a first training in managing a country. He would put this again into practice in Egypt. Indeed, his conception of the expedition went beyond the military and he quite truthfully believed himself to be a new Alexander the Great.

Although raised in the arch-Catholic culture of Corsica, he believed more in his 'star', meaning destiny, than in God. This had two obvious direct impacts on his attitude during the expedition. His decisions were not to be questioned as events would therefore yield to his own plans and vision. The destruction of the fleet at Aboukir Bay, and the siege of Acre, would show the limits of such exuberant confidence. As a gifted mathematician, he also tended to calculates the odds with much disregard to what it may mean for his troops. The other consequence was that his attitude towards Islam throughout his presence in Egypt can at best be called "ambiguous". He supported that faith whenever it was convenient for his own schemes. At the same time, he was keen to nurture relationships with the various indigenous Christian groups, Coptic or Greek. These were natural allies for the French, and they would provide on-going support both in terms of administration (especially levying taxes) or military (Coptic and Greek Legions).

Bonaparte's leadership style is strikingly displayed in the daily orders for the army. Almost not a day passed by without one being issued and therefore read to the troops. The orders ranged from the mundane to the strategic, but all are signs of Bonaparte's hyperactivity, something he would carry on throughout the Consulate and Empire. It is truly hard to consider the Egyptian campaign as a success for Bonaparte. As in Italy, it started with decisive victories. However, the army was far from being as enthusiastic for Egypt as was its leader. The disaster at Aboukir bay led to the Syrian campaign. In typical Napoleonic fashion, this endeavour was too much of a stretch. Ill-prepared logistically, the army was saved by commissary-in-chief Daure's exceptional qualities as he managed to keep supplies flowing and feed the army. Worse, Bonaparte quite plainly under-estimated his adversaries and ultimately lost too many men and some of his very best officers in front of Acre. Yet, again in typical Napoleonic fashion, he managed to spin this quasi-disaster into a quasi-success as he walked back into Cairo. The victory over the Turks at Aboukir enabled him to come out of all this adventure yet again victorious and depart for France, leaving Kléber to clean up his mess. For the rest of his life, Napoleon would look back to Egypt as a key moment in his destiny, but he was, as always, very keen to ensure that it was his view on what had happened would be left for generations to come. During the Consulate, he specifically ordered that documents related to the expedition be burned, including his own. He visibly did not feel all too comfortable as to what could be found in those papers!

There could hardly be someone more different than Bonaparte to follow in his stead. Jean-Baptiste Kléber was Bonaparte's elder by sixteen years. He is, to this day, a legend in his own native region of Alsace. Born in Strasburg within a moderately wealthy urban family, his taste for the military started at an early age. He joined the 1st Hussars (Bercheny) in 1769, the year that Napoleon was born, but left the unit almost immediately at his mother's request to finish his studies. Incredibly gifted as an artist and engineer, he studied in Alsace and Paris and became a full-fledged architect by 1774. At the age of twenty-four, he enrolled again, but this time in the Bavarian army: staying there only for a few months, he then left to take up the rank of privaten-kadet in the Kaunitz Infantry Regiment of Austria. He left the Austrian ranks in 1783, having achieved the rank of second lieutenant in 1779, but with no further hopes of promotion. Although undoubtedly brilliant, his strong temper and non-noble background prevented him from any progression. Also, the period was peaceful and so there was no hope of being distinguished on the battlefield. He resumed his practice as an architect in Alsace with quite some success, being named the chief architect of the town of Belfort on the eve of the French Revolution. It is that event which brought him back, and this time for good, into the military. A true son of the age of enlightenment, Kléber was an early hard-core republican. Like so many other non-nobles with past military experience, he was quickly promoted and in 1793 was already a général de brigade. His defence at the siege of Mayence resulted in his garrison being able to leave with the honours of war.

At the head of these troops he was sent to battle the insurrection in Vendée. He was witness there to the horrors of that civil war while being promoted to général de divison. He was then posted to the Army of the North in 1794 and fought at the successful battle of Fleurus.

As a man whose philosophy combined order and tolerance, he was not an avid supporter of the Robespierre terror regime, but even less of the rather corrupt Directory which replaced it in 1795. Placed, because of his public disapproval of the regime, in semi-retirement, he saw in Bonaparte's expedition an occasion to distance himself from the current government and go back to what he knew best, leading troops on the battlefield.

All witnesses agree on Kléber's personal integrity, ethics, intellectual brilliance, republican ardour, and incredible physical courage. Napoleon on Saint-Helena was to say that 'courage, design, he had everything … it was Mars the god of war personified'. Compared to many other leaders, Kléber lacked personal ambition. An active freemason, his most ardent desire was to see a stable democratic political system put in place in France. He was beloved by his troops and the army at large, as all knew of his personal bravery and care for the common soldier. He was also amazingly eloquent and could in very few words inspire the army in achieving victories.

As he took over the command in Egypt, he was torn between his anger against Bonaparte, who had abandoned the army, and his intense sense of duty. His leadership over the army was immediate and the change was actually more than welcomed by all. The trickier part was to see whether he would command over Egypt and the Egyptians. In that role, he actually revealed himself to be probably more gifted than Bonaparte. Whereas the latter used to ride into Cairo with little to no pomp, escorted mainly by his Guides, Kléber made sure that on the very first day he marched as the new commander into Cairo, he would be preceded by the traditional native guards armed with staffs to clear the way for him. His first encounter with the Egyptian leaders at the Diwan made it very clear for them that he meant business and they all found him much less amiable than Bonaparte. He however perfectly understood the psychology of men as we can tell from his own written notes and reflexions which have survived.

The daily orders issued by Kléber reflect with strength his own command style. Unlike Bonaparte, he would issue an order only if necessary. Typically these are very factual, to the point and short. All his decisions as commander-in-chief could be summarised as putting the welfare and survival of his troops first to ensure they could be brought back to Europe to support the republic against its enemies.

Jacques Menou was the last commander-in-chief of the army of the Orient. Again, there could be no greater contrast in change of leadership. Menou's full name was actually Jacques-François de Menou, Baron de Boussay. Born in 1750 into an ancient noble family dating back to the 11th century, Menou was one of those enlightened noblemen who, early on, supported the Revolution. Like so many other scions of the nobility, he had joined the military and was a maréchal de camp in 1789; in more modern terms, a général de brigade. Promoted to général de divison in 1793, most of his career successes were achieved within the French borders, fighting in the Vendée and then against Parisian insurgents in 1795. Menou had actually very little taste for the military. His true passion was what was then known as 'political economy', i.e. economics. Menou throughout his life and career stands out miscast as an officer, but an able economist or manager. He was also very typical of the liberal nobility of the late 18th century. He combined intellectual curiosity, in his case, economics, with an avid taste for pleasures and his own comfort. Unlike most of the expeditionary force, he saw French Egypt as the possible start of a new colonial domain. In many ways, he was the predecessor of the officers and administrators who would in the 19th century carve out the new French colonial empire. It is debated to this day as to whether his conversion to Islam was a true act of faith or just a means to an end to enable him to marry a young native woman, descendent of the prophet, whom he had fallen in love with. Although an obvious protégé of Bonaparte, his career after Egypt was to be undistinguished and he would encounter the wrath of the new Emperor due to some rather shady financial dealings.

Menou in 1798 by Dutertre. Menou's rather portly appearance is well conveyed by Dutertre and another portrait by him confirms this. He was probably the least military-looking of all the officers in Egypt!

Unsurprisingly both his correspondence and daily orders reflect very much his taste for economics. Unfortunately, his own writing style was far from resembling either Bonaparte's or Kléber's. His prose is lengthy, complex and quite pompous. Menou, as commander-in-chief was to issue such orders on a quasi-daily basis. One cannot but wonder what the troops thought as these were read out to them every day. Compared to Bonaparte's energetic prose and Kléber's morale-boosting words, Menou's long dissertations on currency conversions, fiscal schemes, and other such fascinating topics must have seemed quite dull, and worse, to have fuelled Menou's very poor reputation with his troops. Although he had agreed to seek advice on military matters from his more able fellow generals, his own ego got him quickly into conflict with most of them, all the more so since the most talented one who was left, Reynier, had himself a big ego and a bad temper.

The British invasion of Egypt was not a foregone conclusion. Abercromby's troops were still fairly raw and a few mistakes were made which the French should have been able to benefit from. Yet, Menou's utter incompetence, indecisiveness, and in the end brash decisions led to the disaster at Alexandria/Canope and he then let himself being blocked in Alexandria losing all contact with the rest of his forces in Cairo. It is quite telling that he was never put in charge of troops again, whereas Reynier was.

Beyond the three commanders-in-chief, there lay their immediate circles and beyond that their own subordinates. There is no doubt as to the

# THE FRENCH ARMY OF THE ORIENT 1798–1801

Desaix in 1798 by Dutertre. Desaix' profile portrait is usually a shock to most people familiar with other portraits of Desaix. Rarely shown in profile, Desaix has been 'idealised' in his later portraits. The man, however gifted he was, was certainly no beauty-pageant winner!

quality and talent of their military leadership. True, with Bonaparte's own rise to power and his sense of recognition for those men who had followed him into the Orient, they were to have a distinguished career in the Empire. Yet, Napoleon was no big fan of favourites or nepotism. Without doubt, he would favour friends or family but only if they actually performed and followed his lead.

Out of the 2,500 officers, six were to become marshals of France at some stage during the Empire: Murat, Lannes, Bessières, Berthier, Davout, and Marmont. If the first four were already part of Bonaparte's inner circle, the last two were barely known of Bonaparte then.

Murat had been following Bonaparte since the 'whiff of grapeshot' of 13 Vendémiaire when he had met him and was ordered to bring back guns to put down the royalist insurgency in Paris. He had distinguished himself as an able cavalry leader in Italy, but was only a général de brigade at the start of the Egyptian campaign. The cavalry was at first put under the command of Général de Divison Thomas-Alexandre Dumas, a more senior and accomplished commander. Following Dumas' departure for France, Murat was put in charge of the cavalry and led it through the Syrian campaign and the battle of Aboukir. The rest, as one says, is history: having become one of Bonaparte's closest friends, by the end of 1799, he was the first commander of the newly created consular guard and soon to become his boss' brother-in-law by marrying Caroline Bonaparte in January 1800.

Lannes had started as an uneducated volunteer. Like Murat, and many other officers, he was form the south-west which like Alsace had been traditionally a region which provided soldiers and officers for the French army. Lannes, although self-taught as an officer was naturally gifted in both tactics and strategy and would spend his life honing those skills by constant learning. His well-known and perceivable lack of education made him an easy target for his fellow officers. While cruising for Egypt, on board the *Orient*, Junot would verbally strike out at him while Bonaparte was entertaining discussions with scientists by asking 'where is Lannes?'. Junot would pronounce Lannes' name by insisting deeply on the first syllable making it sound like 'l'âne' – a donkey – which in France is an animal taken as a symbol of stupidity. Lannes would, however, prove far from stupid in Egypt and show his usual physical bravery which would earn him his place on board the return ship with Bonaparte.

Bessières was, of the four, probably the least gifted. A true nobleman and like Murat a former member of the king's constitutional guard, Bessières was to be throughout his life a representative of his caste. A born soldier and rider he was in command of the Guides since the Italian campaign. As such, he was at the head of Bonaparte's personal bodyguard. He would carry that role onwards and be in command of the Consular Guard and later Imperial Guard cavalry.

Berthier needs little to no introduction given his well-known future. His presence and attitude in Egypt need however some explanation. Born into a well-to-do Versailles family close to royal circles, Berthier and his brother César both participated in the American War of Independence on Rochambeau's staff. Supremely gifted in planning and organisation, Berthier shone immediately as Bonaparte's chief of staff in Italy. He especially showed that above all, he could understand Bonaparte's designs and translate them into concise, clear orders. He had thus made himself indispensable to Bonaparte and was the obvious choice as his right hand man for Egypt and also to bring back with him to France. Berthier's mind was however far from clear in Egypt and very much focused on other matters. In Italy he had met the Countess Visconti and had madly fallen in love with her. This was to be the great love of his life. Although this was mutually shared, Visconti was married. The morals of the time being what they were, this did not create however too much of a problem, but distance would. Berthier actually brought with him to Egypt several portraits and tokens of affection from Visconti. It is well recorded that he had set up in his tent or in his lodgings a shrine or altar to his love in front of which he could spend inordinate amounts of time. Bonaparte, and others, quite logically ridiculed his subordinate who was also his elder by sixteen years and at forty-five not exactly a teenager suffering his first true passion.

Davout at only 28 was an ambitious cavalry leader. In charge of Desaix' cavalry during the greater part of the campaign in Upper-Egypt, he would follow him back to France. Desaix' death at Marengo would propel him to the front as Bonaparte ensured that his friend's associates were taken care of (this would also benefit Savary and Rapp who were both ADCs to Desaix). Davout's overall attitude in Egypt is in sharp contrast to what we know of Davout in his later career. He is described by several witnesses as overly ambitious and for that reason rather reckless resulting in unnecessary losses – Lasalle, chef de brigade of the 22nd Chasseurs in Egypt and thus under his direct leadership, especially complained about him.

Marmont had already crossed Bonaparte's path on several occasions. Like him, he was a gifted artilleryman with a sharp intellect and a mercurial character. He distinguished himself at the storming of Malta and was promoted to général de brigade. In Egypt was is mainly in charge of administration and defending Alexandria. Very much trusted by Bonaparte who probably saw in him a reflection of his own self, at least intellectually, he returned back with Bonaparte to France.

Beyond those six who were to have such a brilliant destiny under the Empire, several other officers were to play a major role in future years.

There are those who are directly related to Bonaparte.

First amongst them is Bonaparte's brother Louis. Louis was the only other Bonaparte to have embarked on a military career. An officer of dragoons, he accompanied his brother in Egypt as his ADC. Known for his brooding and difficult character, and of a sickly nature, he left Egypt in March 1799 to bring dispatches back to the Directory.

## THE FRENCH ARMY OF THE ORIENT 1798–1801

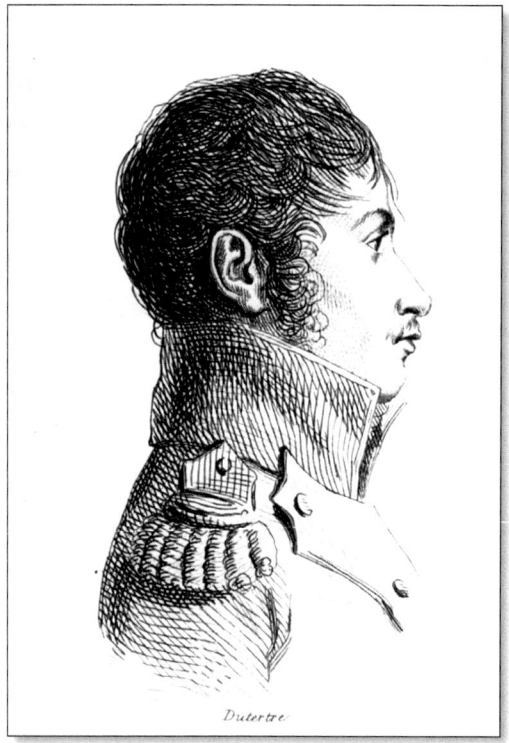

Eugène de Beauharnais by Dutertre. Another rather surprising portrait, as we typically know Eugène better as man in his thirties with a baldish forehead. His profile reminds one of his mother's and he does come across as a youthful teenager.

Eugène de Beauharnais was Bonaparte's stepson. At the age of nineteen he was still a teenager, although this was not his first military campaign. He was one of Bonaparte's ADCs and very much appreciated by him. He was one of the two ADCs charged with negotiating the surrender of the garrison of Jaffa. He naively promised they would have their lives spared and had to suffer the moral consequences of the subsequent mass execution that followed. Bernoyer's letters provide an interesting aspect of Eugène in Egypt. He is described very much as a 'golden boy' enjoying his position and wealth an indulging in the purchasing of a gorgeous black female slave to no other purpose than sexual pleasure.

If Eugène and Louis became Bonaparte's ADCs due to their family ties, Jozef Sulkowski had no personal relationship to Bonaparte other than his friendship and admiration. Indeed Sulkowski was by all accounts Bonaparte's favourite ADC. Of about the same age as Bonaparte, Sulkowski was born in Poland and had fought in the last Polish army against the partition of his country. In 1793 he moved to France, becoming a logical supporter of the French Revolution. Extremely well educated, incredibly gifted in all aspects of science and culture, he was also an accomplished linguist. Having met the great orientalist Venture de Paradis, he became engaged to his daughter and was to be posted to the embassy in Constantinople. Having failed to get there, he joined the French army and fought in Italy where he met Bonaparte. His vast knowledge and excellent military skills logically brought him to follow Bonaparte. He was atrociously killed on the second day of the Cairo insurrection in October 1798. Although having been active only for about three months, Sulkowski managed to leave a lasting impression on all. He contributed several articles to the Egyptian Institute, including a detailed description of the road from Cairo to Salehyeh, and worked on a French-Arab lexicon to be used by the troops.

Outside of Bonaparte's family circle, one man had the privilege of being his friend, Desaix. There were so many similarities between the two that only rivalry or friendship could have developed. Desaix was older than Bonaparte by only a year. Like him, he came from an impoverished noble family from Auvergne in the mountainous centre of France which could trace its nobility back to the 13th century. Like him he was already part of the royal army, and like him had decided to throw his lot with the Revolution rather than to emigrate. By 1794, he was already a général de division given his impeccable service and his impressive military talent. This was the other point they had in common, both were young military geniuses and both recognised and admired the other's talents. Just before the expedition, Desaix had actually toured Bonaparte's Italian battlefields to better understand what he had done. He therefore joined Bonaparte's command, knowing very well who he was following. From that moment on he devoted himself to Bonaparte and became a true friend of his. There was no ambition on the part of Desaix, only that to serve Bonaparte just like a knight of the old days would have followed his king.

Desaix was fortunate enough also to be given an independent command in Upper-Egypt which gave him a lot of leeway and avoided having him witness some of Bonaparte's worst mistakes. Specifically, he did not follow him into Syria which was one of the main reasons which Kléber distanced himself from Bonaparte. Finally Desaix' glorious death at Marengo transformed him into a quasi-martyr as Bonaparte truly grieved his loss. He made sure all of Desaix' relatives were well provided for afterwards and also took with him his ADCs and officers. There is one final interesting anecdote about Desaix. After his death, portraits were made of Desaix, especially one by Andrea Appiani, the well-known Italian painter. This painting became the model for all further images of Desaix. In it he is shown as a clean-shaven handsome young man. Unfortunately, all surviving drawings made by Dutertre and show a very different image of him. Desaix had been severely wounded in the face on several occasions and would hide the scars beneath a thick black moustache. He had a very slopping chin and sharp crooked nose which made him far from an attractive man!

The Army of the Orient would not however have survived if it had not been for some men whose background was not strictly military even though they wore a uniform. More than in any other campaign, the support functions were a critical part of the expedition.

Even before the expedition set on, it was obvious that medical services would play an important part in the campaign. The doctors, surgeons, and pharmacists who followed were both essential to the military operations but were also, in their own way, scientists who were eager to discover Egypt from a medical angle. Both Desgenettes who was chief medical officer of the army and Larrey who was chief surgeon were to attain lasting medical fame and have a distinguished career later on. Desgenettes was already a confirmed doctor when he joined the army. A nobleman with a deep sense of his duties as a medical practitioner, he ended up several times at odds with Bonaparte. He voluntarily injected himself with purulent liquid from a man who was recovering the plague in Jaffa to show to the troops they need not be so afraid of it. In another but different display of courage, he refused to obey Bonaparte's order to put to permanent sleep the sick in Jaffa when the army was retreating. Desgenettes was also a close friend of Kléber and left in an anonymous publication *Souvenirs of a Doctor of the Expedition to Egypt*, several notes and quotes he had heard from him. He also wrote an official medical history of the Army of the Orient. Larrey was by all accounts the master surgeon of his days. Incredibly gifted in his art, his career extended up to Waterloo and beyond. Like Desgenettes, his work in Egypt largely fed his own memoirs of which a good part is actually highly technical. Both Desgenettes and Larrey were very active in ensuring the wounded and sick would be well tended to – even proposing and putting in place an ambulance carried by camels.

Of all the men of science who joined the army in Egypt, Nicolas Conté is probably the least well-known but also the man who had the greatest (positive) impact on the expedition.

Unlike many, Conté was a true son of the lower classes. He was born in 1755 into a family of farmers but showed exceptional gifts very early on for both drawing and mechanical engineering. Before the Revolution, he was making a living as a portrait painter, but saw then the opportunity to go back to what he liked most: mechanical and chemical engineering. The list of his own inventions quickly became endless and he was put in charge by the Revolutionary government of organising the military balloon corps. It was in this role as well as head of the 'mechanical workshop' that he joined the expedition. As most of the balloon equipment was lost at Aboukir Bay, he concentrated himself on managing the workshop. With supplies from France being cut off, the workshop and Conté quickly became indispensable. Any problems that came up were proposed to Conté and his men, and he usually would come up with a solution. Drawing on the craftsmanship of the native Egyptians he set up weapons factories, turning out sabres, firearms, and gunpowder. According to Monge, himself a scientific genius, 'Conté had all the sciences in his head and all the arts in his hands'. Some of his design" would be retained for later use, like the cavalry musket which became an official regulation pattern as of Year IX in France. Still an artist, Conté also documented what he was seeing and some of his watercolours have survived and are a precious testimonial of life in Egypt.

Last amongst the staff support functions was the war commissary. In charge of all supplies, this department had the life of the army in its hands. It was first headed up by de Sucy, who had the same function in Italy, but aged, tired, and unwilling to bear with all the difficulties facing the army he decided to return to France and was replaced by Hector Daure on 21 November 1798. At only 26 years of age, Daure was already a confirmed commissary and whereas some have military, artistic, or scientific gifts, Daure was a financial and business wizard. Supremely well organised, capable of handling several issues at the same time, Daure, despite his young age, filled his role with more than just competence. His highest point came when, marching with the army into Syria, he managed to feed it, despite all the adverse conditions.

Daure's correspondence with all the various departments and general officers was handed over by his family to the French war archives and they can be consulted there. They are a major source to understand how the army managed to operate and specifically how it was dressed and equipped. Daure was to continue his career into the Empire, reaching a high point when becoming the minister of finance of the kingdom of Naples under Murat. However Daure's ambition was such, that in the process he also became Queen Caroline's lover. Not that Murat harboured deadly resentment for this as both him and his wife were known to be fairly promiscuous, but there was a line not to be crossed when being a minister of the King of Naples and Daure was sent back to France. In 1815, Daure was the chief quartermaster of the Army of the North, thus ensuring the supply of Napoleon's last campaign. He was to continue his career under the restoration given his well-known competence.

Under Daure were all the war commissaries. These men would be nicknamed by Napoleon's grand army troops as 'rice-bread-salt' after the staple of a soldier's food supply and were never very popular. They were often accused of being at best incompetent, at worst crooks. In the French war archives, there is a document, probably established under Menou when the war commissaries were to be evaluated to be become review inspectors. Some of the comments are quite telling, and direct:

'knows accounting very well'
'activity, zeal and quite a veteran'
'gifted, sharp, a bit lazy'
'knows his job well, but the rigidity of his character ensures he has many enemies'
'excellent war commissary, honest and hard working'
'distinguished individual, well educated, honest and well trained'
'not fit for his job'
'bad war commissary'
'better suited for the military than for administrative duties'

On another document some precise comments are made – do note that these comments are put in front of a 'qualities' column which for all these individuals state either 'very strong' or 'strong':

'arch-revolutionary'
'was in forced labour and was recently put under arrest by General Rampon as he had sold 19 oxen and accepted their payment in front of the troops'
'a total ignorant crook'
'was ADC to Generals Bon and Davout who both have got rid of him because he had stolen from them'
'the only thing is that he does like a drink or two'

Indeed part of the advantages of the role of a war commissary was that he could potentially make a profit out of his function. In some cases, disciplinary action was taken, but at that time, sanctions were fairly light. Under Napoleon, misconduct by a war commissary could bring him in front of a firing squad as the Emperor knew all too well these men were despised by the troops and such a decision always proved popular with them!

## Officers, and Men

What of the lower ranks? Compared to the general officers and staff, we have much less material to draw on, but given the adventure they lived through, some left memoirs or notes. All too often, these were written much later and are not always an immediate testimonial of their experience in Egypt.

They were typically young men from a rural background. Such is the case for: Joseph Laporte born in 1780 in Grenoble, an NCO in the 1st battalion of the 69th Demi-Brigade who left a recently published narration *Mon voyage en Égypte et en Syrie* (*My Voyage in Egypt and Syria*); Jean-Claude Vaxelaire, from the Vosges-Lorraine region, born in 1770 and carabinier in the 2nd Light Demi-Brigade and who wrote his *Histoire d'un veteran de l'ancienne armée (History of a Veteran of the Old Army)* for his children and grandchildren; Pierre Millet born in 1776 in Normandy, chasseur in the 21st Light Demi-Brigade who also left memoirs, *Souvenirs de la campagne d'Égypte (Memoirs of the Campaign in Egypt)*. In both these last cases, these accounts were found and published by descendants of the authors.

But these are the men who made it, went home and were proud to retell their stories, even if, at times they would gladly embellish them. Such is also the case of the memoirs of Captain François, nicknamed the Egyptian dromedary. François was captured at the very end of the expedition to France and got back to France only much later to join the war in the Spain and then Waterloo. François' odyssey throughout the Orient, although very picturesque, is filled with tall tales with him seducing harem women, escaping slavery and so on.

Much more interesting are the small snippets about the common men which one can find reading through the daily orders. After the sinking of the fleet, army morale degraded and men started to desert. Thus, the daily orders give many details about these desperate men, eager to escape the vicissitudes of the Egyptian campaign.

> Joseph Mischoute, 75th Line Demi-Brigade, from Malta, 24 years old, 1.60m tall
>
> Dominique Gersoni from Naples, grenadier sergeant, 2nd battalion, 18th Line Demi-Brigade, 24 years old, 1.70m tall
>
> Jean-Baptiste Picard, gunner 1st class, 11th Company 4th Artillery, black hair and beard, blue eyes average face, 1,71m tall
>
> Vincent Gray, from Malta, 18th Dragoons, 1.66m tall
>
> Claude Alsouparde from Malta, 18th Dragoons, 1.72m tall
>
> Pierre Dergalle from Le Mans, 18th Dragoons, 1.66m tall
>
> Jean-Barthélémi Maurot, drummer 22nd Light Demi-Brigade, 1.60m tall
>
> Joseph Perau, 19 years of age, 1.60m tall, 18th Line Demi-Brigade
>
> Simon Carneja, 21 years of age, 1.70m tall, 18th Line Demi-Brigade

Without being exhaustive, these give us a glimpse into the actual men who composed the troops. Those whose details are listed are young, typically in their late teens or early twenties. Many actually come from the south of France or Italy, although many other French regions were represented. As the campaign dragged on, many Maltese troops were incorporated into regular French units. Their average height is much lower than one would expect. The typical size for a grenadier of 1.76m seems to be more the exception than the rule – incidentally this is currently the average height for a modern Frenchman.

# THE MEN AND THEIR DAILY LIFE

They were not necessarily dishonest, unruly, or without morals, yet the conditions which they faced in Egypt probably forced them more than once to be violent and immoral. In the mind-set of the time, they did not see necessarily any evil in their attitude. The culture shock, as we say today, was too great for them to bear and only the more enlightened, the scientists and some of the officers, managed to cope with it.

To finish off with the men, here is a very moving letter from a desperate mother sent from her home in Riom, Auvergne, central France, in early February 1800.

> A mother quite worried as to the fate of one of her sons dares have you listen to her plight.
> 
> Citizen Laroche, a lieutenant in the Guides of General Bonaparte followed him to Egypt after having kissed his parents and told them of Generals Bonaparte and Berthier of his love and respect for such leaders all the while trying to lay aside the grief of separation, all the more cruel as the dangers might be great.
> 
> My son told us letters would be difficult to get and uncertain. We received only one letter at the beginning of the victories in Egypt since then we received new only indirectly et that has not been enough to quiet our fears.
> 
> A general such as you cannot ignore the fate of such an officer – Citizen Minister; this is what I have been telling myself since you have returned. But I did not dare ask you for this until this day as the greater common interest is such that it should not yield to that of an individual, however important it might be. Today your tasks are no less important, but maybe you can tell me something about my son. Please forgive a mother's intrusion as she has three sons in the service of our homeland. One supports and shares the glory of the garrison in Malta, and I sometimes have news of him. He too followed General Bonaparte. The general in charge of the defence of this island has kept my older son as one of his ADCs.
> 
> My third son has joined the 9th Hussars last year as he barely reached the required age of 18.
> 
> But my second son does not give us news from Egypt. Citizen Minister, you know what had become of him when you left those shores. Please let a family know as its patriotic devotion is worthy of your care and interest

So, what had happened to Lieutenant Laroche? Had he been wounded or died? The letter which can be found in the administrative archives box of the Guides does not have an answer attached to it. Luckily, the fate of all there brothers can easily be traced and is worthy of telling as it is so typical of the period, with two of them having been involved with the Egyptian expedition.

Pierre-Victor Laroche was the son who was so much worrying his mother. He was born in Riom in 1774. His father was a prosecutor at the court of Auvergne and at the court of Riom. The family background was therefore urban, well-to-do, and probably very well-known within the Auvergne region. They probably backed the Revolution and Pierre-Victor joined as a volunteer in 1791. From then until April 1795, he was an infantryman, ending up in the 54th Demi-Brigade. He then joined the 7th *bis* Hussars and transferred to the Guides of the Army of Italy on 5 March 1796. He participated in the Italian campaign and quickly rose through the ranks to become a second lieutenant in the Guides in May 1797. He was promoted to first lieutenant on 22 August 1798, captain on 12 September 1799 and squadron commander on 19 August 1801. He distinguished himself at Heliopolis and Korain in March 1800. He was not listed as one of the Guides officers coming back to France, as he had then transferred to his new unit, the 18th Dragoons. He stayed there until December 1803 when he moved to the 5th Dragoons. He became a major in that regiment in 1804 and then colonel of the 13th Dragoons on 20 September 1806 at the age of 32 and after 15 years of service. He was awarded the legion of honour in the first promotion of 1804 and was made an officer of the order in 1807. He was made a baron of the empire in 1808, when titles of nobility were re-instated. He fought with the Grand Army in the campaigns of 1805, 1806 and 1807. As of 1808 he was in Spain with his regiment where he died of 'putrid fever' on 18 December 1809 at 7pm.

The older son is also named Pierre-Victor but was born in 1769. He was a second lieutenant in the 8th Hussars in 1792 and a captain in that regiment (renumbered as the 7th) by 1794. He fought in the Vendée and then on the Rhine and transferred into the 7th *bis* in March 1795 as a captain – so it was probably him who brought his younger brother into the unit. He fought in Italy and then is indeed an ADC to General Vaubois in Malta. He came back to France after the surrender of the garrison and transferred to the Franco-Dutch army with the rank of squadron commander. He remained a squadron commander up to 1808, in the 10th and then 15th Dragoons. He was promoted a major in the Tuscan Dragoons regiment which became the 28th Chasseurs and became its colonel in 1811 at the age of 42. Tired and worn out by campaigning, he became a junior review inspector in 1813 and finally abandoned the service due to illness in March 1815. He died in Riom in September 1816. He was awarded the legion of honour in 1804 and made a knight of the Empire in 1809.

The last son was Jean-Baptiste Laroche, born in 1778. After being in the 9th Hussars from 1798 to 1801, he joined the Chasseurs of the Guard in 1801 and left them in 1805 to become a second lieutenant in the 9th Dragoons, promoted first lieutenant in 1807, then aide-major in the 28th Chasseurs in 1809. Once again the eldest of the Laroches brought with him one of his brothers. He became a captain in 1810 and left for the 11th Chasseurs in 1814. In 1816, he was a captain of the Chasseurs de l'Oise. He was awarded the legion of honour in 1814, but no other document in the legion of honour archives can help trace what happened to him afterwards. Like his brothers he had fought with the Grand Army in Germany, Prussia, Poland, Spain, but also Russia and then France – all this having suffered only one wound back in 1799!

### Sex, Drugs, and Rocks

In all the books that have been written on the Egyptian campaign the topic of daily life is addressed – therefore the following paragraphs have no pretension other than providing some background and a few lesser-known anecdotes.

As the men set foot in July 1798 on the sands of Aboukir Bay, many of them knew of Egypt. Their enthusiasm and excitement was genuine. This was the late 18th century, the time of neo-classicism. Officers had been raised reading their classics, admiring Caesar and Mark-Anthony, dreaming of Cleopatra's beauty and, above all, as young military men, dreaming to emulate the greatest hero of all times, Alexander the Great. In their memoirs, almost all men recall that, as they walked towards Alexandria, they thought of him and the fabled city which bore his name. But, as they captured and entered it, their disappointment was all the more bitter. Alexandria in 1798 was a squalid town with none of its former glory. All mention the shabbiness of the buildings, the filthy streets, and the stray dogs.

After this, came the walk across the desert. The first clashes with the Mamelukes, the brutal murder of any straggling man, and then Cairo which looked barely better than Alexandria.

Again dogs walked freely about the streets and at night time would fill the air with loud barking. It became too much even for the cool Bonaparte who ordered that the dogs be slain. After having killed Mamelukes, the troops went on a canine rampage.

Then there were the locals. Bonaparte had issued a stern daily order before disembarking telling his troops to respect the people and their main religion, Islam. If the Egypt of ancient times spoke to the French, the Muslim religion at best reminded some of the crusades. The ferocity of the first Cairo insurrection, the fighting against 'mogrehbins' from Mecca presented them with a harsh reality which even some of the local Egyptian leaders had trouble understanding. If the mid to late 18th century had seen a Christian revival in Protestant countries with Methodism, Islam was also enjoying a re-birth with the emergence of Wahhabism. This variant of the Muslim faith was then in full growth and had started to reach Egypt. The French were not faced with one enemy, the Mamelukes, but with three. Indeed the Mamelukes wanted power back, as did the Turks, but then there were those who saw themselves as fighting the miscreants, many coming from North Africa or the Arabian Peninsula.

Despite attempts at bridging the cultural gap, the French never really took on root in Egypt. They ended up relying on local Christian communities like the Copts and the Greeks, alienating both themselves and those populations from the vast majority of locals. There were, oddly enough, a few conversions to the Muslim faith. The most prominent is of course that of General Menou. It is still to be debated as to his sincerity, and indeed, as a liberal free-thinker, Menou probably agreed to his conversion only to bed his future wife.

Only the scientists felt probably truly at home as their task proved huge and they were deeply immersed into it. As the French left Egypt, they did leave behind a number of innovations which had shaken the Egyptian society and would lead on to modern Egypt. Conversely, the French had had first-hand experience of the Orient and the few lessons learned would not be lost after 1830 when France gradually built up a new colonial empire in North Africa.

The shock was not only of culture, but also of climate. Nothing had really prepared the army for the intense sun and heat it would face, nor the cold desert nights. The intense sunlight was however the main problem the French would face during their stay. All memoirs, letters, and reports are filled with

# THE FRENCH ARMY OF THE ORIENT 1798–1801

Madame Verdier by Dutertre. General Verdier's wife as she appeared in Egypt is known to us through this portrait and an oil painting showing her in 7th *bis* Hussar outfit sharing a canteen of water with a soldier. In the painting she looks like a fairly good-looking woman in her thirties with light coloured hair. Dutertre's portrait is far less flattering and shows more of an ageing Italian matron. As one soldier put it 'all women, even the less pleasant looking became beauties given the lack of their kind in Egypt'.

mentions of cases of ophthalmia, some temporary and others resulting in permanent blindness.

The other major health hazard was of course what was known generically as 'plague'. It is difficult two hundred years down to assess if all the epidemics mentioned are indeed of bubonic plague, but we know for sure that on several occasions, including at Jaffa, that this was indeed the case.

Filth and simply poor overall sanitary conditions also proved a major challenge. Fortunately, the army had some of the best medical minds of its time with the likes of Desgenettes and Larrey. Larrey's time in Egypt was not lost on him and much of his medical memoirs, published in 1812, relate to the observations he made in Egypt. It was also in such conditions that Larrey started developing fast field ambulances, adapting stretchers on to camels to ensure the wounded could be swiftly brought to the dressing stations.

The French soldiers of the Revolution and Empire were known to be brave, but also to know how to have fun and to please their usually unwilling hosts. One can most certainly debate the reality behind such reputation. Most of the men of the Army of the Orient had been part of the Italian campaign. In Italy, outside of the hard campaigning days, the French had a rather leisurely life. Italy was rich, its population rather welcoming. Women were especially noted for their beauty and rather unequivocal approach to fraternisation with French troops. Some of the highest ranks of the French army had benefited from such pleasures. General Verdier was to bring to Egypt his Italian wife, and Berthier fond memories of Countess Visconti.

Bonaparte had assumed the army would find ample supply of food and beverages, but also women in Egypt. Given the limited space on board the ships, female presence had been more than limited to a few cases and the absolutely necessary laundry women. The general-in-chief had given the example by leaving his wife Josephine behind. We are dealing here with a full-fledged army composed of rather virile individuals, many of good Latin stock with a rather hot temper and with the vast majority between the age of 18 and 40. As one should expect there was a dire need of female presence (to put things mildly) once the troops had landed in Egypt after a good two months of sea travel and just a small respite in Malta. The first contacts in Alexandria were far from conclusive with many mentioning the 'ugliness' of local women. When, that is, one could actually get to see their faces. As the troops crossed on to Cairo, it was too much for some. As Miot relates in his memoirs, some of his commissary colleagues stumbled across the home of an old Egyptian who had a harem of a few 'acceptable' women. Having knocked down the elderly husband and locked him up, the men rushed on to the women – only to find out that they had each been fitted with a chastity belt!

# THE MEN AND THEIR DAILY LIFE

Once in Cairo and with the Mamelukes defeated, the sexual situation improved marginally. As many memoirs mention, as part of the loot, the senior Mamelukes' harems were split between the senior French officers. In the end all 'the good ones' ended up with the highest ranking individuals, the rest being left off for the more junior men. The few European women which were in Cairo, either having resided there as part of the small European community or as part of the expedition, all soon became an obsession for the mass of women-hungry men. As one officer remembers, even the least desirable woman became the subject of fierce seduction efforts,. One such woman, who had been smuggled on board one of the transport ship by her husband, Lieutenant Fourés, as they had just been married was indeed a very attractive young woman. Pauline Fourés was quickly noticed by Bonaparte himself who had finally come to the realisation his own wife Josephine was probably far from been faithful. He whisked her husband away on a mission back to France, and Pauline became the first true official mistress in a long line of mistresses which Bonaparte and then Napoleon was to entertain. Nicknamed 'Belilotte' (a contraption of 'belle idiote' – 'beautiful idiot') or 'Clioupatre' (a variation on Cleopatra) by the troops, she was not part of Bonaparte's return ship. This clearly indicates that she was more of an enjoyable derivation than a true calling. Yet, as ambitious as she lacked intellect, once back in France she tried to re-kindle her love affair with the new leader of France. She was rather sharply sent away, yet provided for. After one failed marriage, and affair with another officer, she finally married a former Imperial Guard officer and died at the ripe age of 91 in 1869 – probably one of the last surviving witnesses of the Egyptian expedition!

A space within Cairo had been transformed into a pleasure park called 'Tivoli'. There men could indulge in drinking, gambling, and womanising. As usual this could end into brawls and there were a few. But for the greater majority of the rank and file, the one recourse was prostitution. The risk for the women indulging into this with the French was high. French war archives abound with reports of women having been found drowned in the Nile after having been thrown into it in a closed bag. Yet, we have evidence prostitution flourished sometimes in the oddest of places. The French had built a wooden pyramid in the centre of Ezbekieh Sqaure for the yearly celebration of the Republic. The wooden construction was left standing and it provided a comfortable hiding place for paid nightly activities. It came to such a point of scandal that the French Cairo garrison commander had it destroyed.

There was another paid way for young men to indulge in female contact and quite simply it was through purchasing slaves. Again, as odd as it may seem for such vibrant revolutionaries, some turned to this solution. Bernoyer writes vibrant not to say shocking pages on this to his cousin (and obviously not to his wife!), mentioning his purchase of a slave for the sole purpose of sexual entertainment.

One question which has been less well addressed in the various studies published is that of homosexuality. Whereas womanising was tolerated and even glorified, even in the prudish late 19th and early 20th centuries, this alternate sexual practice was not even mentioned as definitely not worthy of the image of the brave, proud, virile French soldier. Yet, it existed, but the testimonials are scant. Unpublished manuscript memoirs in the Orleans public library clearly speak of some officers who would indulge in this, especially with young boys. Rumours have had it that Bonaparte would have had some experience in Egypt, but there is absolutely no ground to this and smells more of slander. In the case of Kléber the topic is more debatable, In St Helena, Napoleon spoke of his chief of staff, Damas, as being his minion and having an undue influence on him. What is certain is that Kléber had many affairs with women. He is supposed to have entertained a relationship with General Verdier's wife and the same manuscript memoirs from Orleans describe quite graphically Kléber practicing sodomy with the wife of the Greek leader Barthelemy.

Aside of the scientists who could not get enough of Egypt, its landscape, animals, and antique stones, the army gradually dragged down into despair. Having hoped on several occasions it would sail back to France, after Kléber's death and under Menou's inept leadership morale sank to all-time low. It is therefore not surprising that in the fall of 1800, Menou had to issue a daily order forbidding the use of the 'liquor of haschich'. These well-known two pages also lash out against the use of strong liquor and clearly show that a sizeable portion of the army had lapsed into addictions, escaping into artificial paradises. This is probably one of the first mentions of addictive drugs in the modern western world and this would be one of the items brought back to Europe, soon to be popular amongst romantic artists.

Such were the men and their life during those three years. The events they saw did mark them for life and many, even in the lower ranks, took the time to write them down or would never miss the opportunity to evoke them.

3

# Doing Much with Little: Organisation and Tactics

Given the nature of the Army of the Orient, this chapter is divided between the organisation of regular army units that made up the original expeditionary force and that of specially-raised units which were specific to that army.

**The Infantry – Initial Organisation**
In 1798, the French army had been waging war for the past six years. Initially composed of the old royal army, it had gradually incorporated various volunteer revolutionary forces, while at the same time losing some of its original structures. The most drastic changes had happened in the infantry. There, the denomination of regiment had given place to a new name: demi-brigade or half-brigade. In essence this was fairly simple to understand. The grouping of two demi-brigades (regiments) formed a brigade, under the command of a général de brigade or brigade general. The regular or line infantry units were named demi-brigade de bataille (battle, or line, half-brigade) and the light infantry units, demi-brigade légère (light half-brigade).

Regular light infantry was a very recent notion in the French army. After having experienced with many light corps during the multiple wars of the first half of the 18th century, France had formalised them by forming legions of chasseurs. These legions combined both foot and mounted troops. The mounted elements had been separated to form the horse chasseurs (chasseurs à cheval), while the foot chasseurs formed fourteen battalions. In 1793, they were given the same organisation as the line infantry, forming the light infantry (infanterie légère). The same year, they had traded their full dark green uniforms for a full dark blue uniform, which they were to keep throughout the period.

All infantry units, light or line, had been constituted by merging former royal regiments with volunteer units through two 'amalgamations'. This makes it rather complex to trace back the origin of any unit of that period.

Let us take the example of the 9th Line Demi-Brigade, Pepin's famous unit which fought in Egypt. It was amalgamated on 4 January 1796 by combining the 2nd Line Demi-Brigade and the 1st and 3rd battalions of the 161st Line Demi-Brigade, units which had themselves been created by the earlier of the two amalgamations on 21 February 1793. The 2nd Line Demi-Brigade had been constituted of the 2nd battalion of the old 1st regiment (Colonel-Général), the 4th Volunteer Battalion of the Somme, and the 5th Volunteer Battalion of Paris. The 161st, in turn was made up of the 1st battalion of the old 89th regiment (Royal-Suédois), the 9th Volunteer Battalion of the North, and the Parisian Molière Volunteers. On paper this represented six battalions, but the way this had been done, veterans of the royal army were aligned with raw volunteers into three battalions. The logic was that the old trained soldiers would bring experience to the younger ones, and in turn these would instil revolutionary fervour into their elders. By all accounts, the system worked and produced the victorious units which fought on the Rhine and in Italy.

The main tactical unit considered throughout the period (1792-1815) for the infantry is the battalion. Like in Britain, a battalion could be separated from its parent unit and operate independently. However, this was much less frequent than in Britain, especially during the pre-Napoleonic period. However, as the reader will see, such orphan battalions participated in the original expeditionary force.

Most demi-brigades had three battalions. Each battalion was composed of one grenadier and eight fusilier companies. In light infantry units, one carabinier and eight chasseur companies. The grenadiers and carabiniers represented the elite of the infantry. They were to be picked amongst the best, bravest, tallest men. They were expected to behave accordingly on or off duty. The minimum height requirement was 1.759m for grenadiers and 1.705m for carabiniers. Up to the consular period, the minimum height to join the army was 1.598m, and the minimum age was eighteen and the maximum forty. Recruits and volunteers were to be single, unmarried, or widowed with no children to support. In practice much of the above was not always followed. For the age, some volunteers cheated on it, enrolling as early as fifteen or sixteen. Revolutionary fervour had also brought into the army some older men. For the size, there were many exceptions. Excellent soldiers whose bravery, strength, and good conduct had distinguished would be transferred to the elite companies even if not meeting the minimum height requirement. It is also worth noting that over time the minimum size could only but be forced to decrease. Up to the mid-1780s, the economic conditions had been fairly good in France. However, the combined effects of the post-American War of Independence depression and harsh winters had resulted in a significant drop in food supply and overall living standards. The chaos which the Revolution had brought exacerbated this. The result was that the average height of a young Frenchman dropped significantly. By 1811, the minimum required had dropped to 1.48m. Although this was not yet the case, even in 1798 an eighteen year old recruit would have been born in 1780, and his entire teenage years would have been spent in the rough Revolutionary period.

A simple fusilier or chasseur would earn 10 sols per day, whereas a grenadier or carabinier would make an extra 1 sol and 6 deniers on top. This higher pay (haute paie), and several differences in dress and equipment, set the grenadiers and carabiniers apart from the regular soldier. These elite

# DOING MUCH WITH LITTLE: ORGANISATION AND TACTICS

The French squares at the Battle of the Pyramids. Detail from an original watercolour by Lucien Rousselot. It very adequately shows how the French infantry, formed in squares with artillery at the angles of the squares, was able to systematically defeat Mameluke cavalry charges.

soldiers were very jealous of such distinctions and we shall see how much they were to hang on to them in Egypt.

On paper a grenadier or carabinier company would have the following organisation

1 Captain (capitaine)
1 Lieutenant (lieutenant or lieutenant en premier)
1 Second Lieutenant (sous-lieutenant or lieutenant en second)
1 Sergeant-Major (sergent-major)
2 Sergeants (sergents)
1 Quartermaster-corporal (caporal-fourrier)
4 Corporals (caporaux)
2 Drummers (tambours)
64 Grenadiers (grenadiers)
This gave a paper total of 83.

A fusilier or chasseur company had a very similar setup except that it had a slightly higher number of men and NCOs.

1 Captain (capitaine)
1 Lieutenant (lieutenant or lieutenant en premier)
1 Second Lieutenant (sous-lieutenant or lieutenant en second)
1 Sergeant-Major (sergent-major)
4 Sergeants (sergents)
1 Quartermaster-corporal (caporal-fourrier)
8 Corporals (caporaux)
2 Drummers (tambours)
104 Fusiliers (grenadiers)
This gave a paper total of 123.

A battalion thus lined up 1,067 men. A demi-brigade, excluding its headquarters would on paper have a total of 3,230 men in its three battalions.

The company was actually an administrative unit. For tactical purposes the company was named a 'peloton' (platoon). This platoon headed up by the captain was then divided into two 'sections' (sections). These were further organised into four 'escouades' (squads).

The first section was led by the lieutenant, the second by the second lieutenant. One sergeant would command the first two squads, a second the next two squads. The third sergeant in the fusiliers or chasseurs companies would be posted to defend the battalion flag which was carried by one sergeant-major designated by the brigade commander. Thus the flag was surrounded by eight sergeants. Each battalion had its own flag, which is fairly logical as technically one battalion could operate independently from the others and needed one therefore as a rallying point and to ensure unit cohesion. Each of the four squads was commanded by a corporal with the support of one chosen man. The fusiliers or chasseurs were to be split as equally as possible between the four squads.

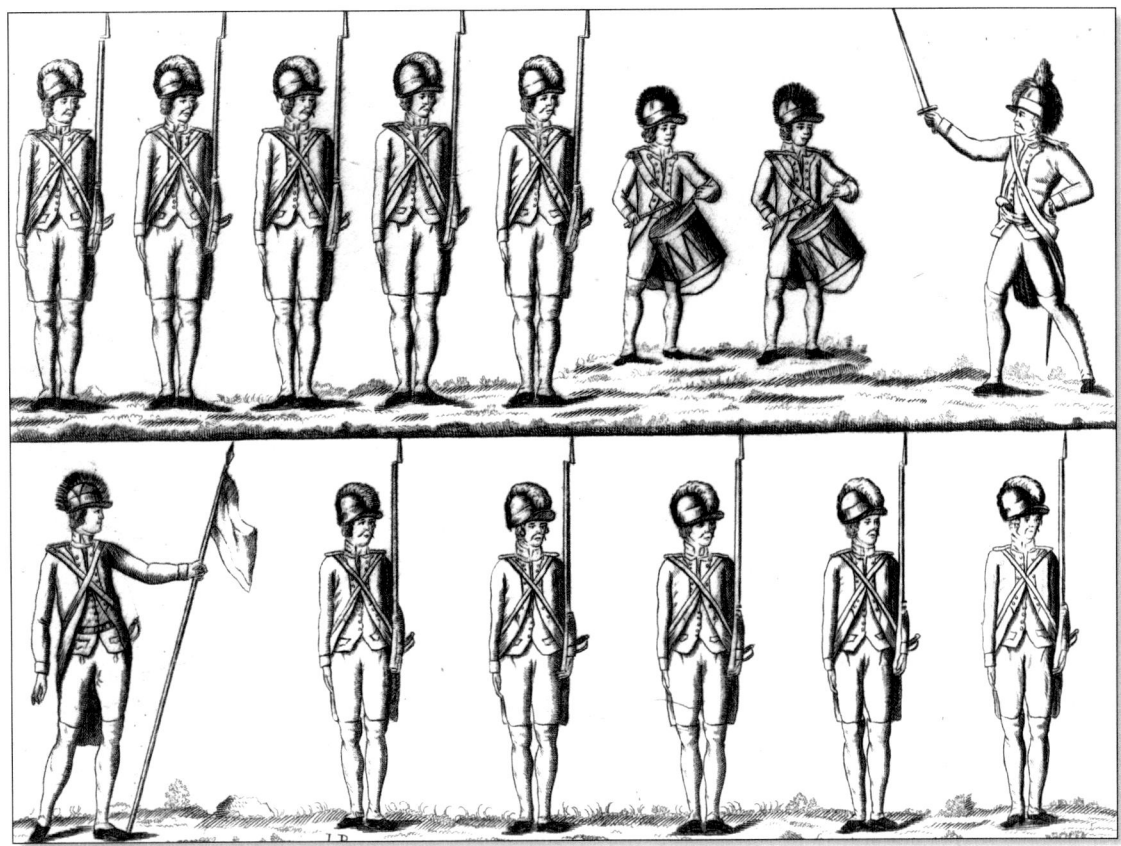

An infantry section. This Revolutionary-period engraving shows a small section of infantry with two drummers, an officer, and what looks to be an NCO with an alignment (section) flag. Note that all men are wearing the 1791 pattern helmet which probably inspired the Egyptian cap.

The grouping of two platoons formed tactically what was known as a division (not to be confused with the divisional grouping of brigades). All these terms were used throughout the infantry exercises and manoeuvre regulations of 1791 which formed the backbone of infantry tactics throughout the Napoleonic period and beyond.

The head of the demi-brigade was no longer named a colonel, a distinction which had disappeared along with the regiment title, but as chef de brigade (brigade commander). In some ways, this was odd as in absolute logic it should have been 'chef de demi-brigade' – but the French Revolutionary had many other such inconsistencies.

The headquarter staff of a demi-brigade was composed as follows:

1 Brigade Commander (chef de brigade)
3 Battalion Commanders (chefs de bataillon)
3 Majors (adjudants-majors)
1 Quartermaster (quartier-maître)
3 Surgeons (chirurgiens)
3 Adjudants (adjudants)
1 Drum-Major (Tambour-Major)
1 Drum Corporal (Caporal Tambour)
8 Musicians (musiciens)
3 Armorers (armuriers)

1 Chief Tailor (tailleur en chef)
1 Chief Cobbler (cordonnier en chef)
A total of 29 men.

So overall a fully staffed demi-brigade fielded on paper 3,259 men. This was of course, never the case. Most units were never at complete strength. Of the four light demi-brigades and eleven line brigades belonging to the Army of the Orient only the 21st Light with 2,000 men and the 13th Line with 2,430 men were the closest to the full figure. Most were in the 1,500-1,800 strength range.

The adjudant-majors were ranked as the equivalent of captains. Their role had been clearly defined in 1791 as being a support to the senior officers in matters of administration, discipline, instruction, and police. Although their scope could cover on some topics the entire unit, they were to focus first and foremost on the battalion to which they were attached. The quartermaster was mainly the treasurer of the unit to whom all matters of finance and supply was to go to. The adjudants were the most senior of all NCOs. They commanded to all other NCOs. Just like for the adjudants-majors their focus was on service, police, and discipline and they supported them and the senior officers in this. The master craftsmen, armorer, tailor and cobbler were essential to the unit in the field. They were there to ensure all possible minor repairs, or, as we shall see at some point in Egypt to ensure manufacturing of clothing and equipment.

The surgeons were likewise essential. Their status throughout the Napoleonic period was fairly ambiguous. They did not rank officially as officers, yet enjoyed some of their prerogatives and were assimilated with them in many respects. On the other hand this lack of official recognition mean they could not partake into some of the privileges officers enjoyed. In the Revolutionary period this was not so much an acute problem as it was to become once officers were fairly easily granted the legion of honour or other such rewards which were typically denied to medical staff. In Egypt, the medical service had an even greater role than in previous campaigns given the very harsh conditions the army encountered. Furthermore, the army-level medical staff was of a very high calibre with the likes of Larrey and Desgenettes and they expected much from their subordinates at the unit level.

The drum-major commanded to both drummers and musicians. He usually had no training to lead a band, but from a command structure standpoint, it made full sense. He had a full and direct leadership on the drum-corporal and drummers. He and the drum-corporal were expected to ensure training of the drummers. Drummers were the period equivalent of modern unit level radio communications. In the clash of battle, orders were best given via the strong beating of the drums. In addition this would give rhythm to some movements and had a definite moral impact on the opposing side. Drummers were not always boys, but often adult soldiers who would keep their cool in the midst of combat and effectively beat the orders. Over time, in Egypt, those veteran drummers would be moved on to other roles and be replaced either by young soldiers or, increasingly by native recruits.

# DOING MUCH WITH LITTLE: ORGANISATION AND TACTICS

Such native replacements were to become rather commonplace. By mid-1798, Desaix was instructed by Bonaparte to 'purchase niggers' (Bonaparte's own written words) from Darfur. This along with other salve purchases in Egypt reinforced the units, especially the 21st Light Demi-Brigade. When the French left Egypt, those men who had survived were to follow. Memoirs from men and officers of the future Imperial army witnessed some in the invasion army on the channel coast in 1804 and later at the siege of Danzig in 1806!

The number of eight musicians may seem low, but this had been more or less the regulation figure for some time and was to stay on into the Empire. In some cases, the officers of a unit would finance musicians beyond the regulation amount. Musicians had a peculiar status. They were not enlisted men as such but can best be described as private contractors. They were artists who would sign a contract with the staff of a unit. Given this, they could be dismissed or, conversely, resign almost at will. Compared to the latter Imperial period, we have few facts related to them during the Revolutionary Wars. We do have some iconography which can help in understanding the composition of a typical Revolutionary period infantry band.

1 Oboe
2 French Horns
1 Fife
2 Clarinets
1 Pair of Cymbals
1 Bass Drum

In addition, a contemporary image shows a young boy holding a triangle and the band being led by the drum-major. Within the eight musicians, one was the band leader (quite often a clarinet player). The band, along with the grouped drummers, was to be led by the drum-major on parade. He headed up the column followed by the drums with the drum-corporal and then the band.

We know for fact that the infantry units which went to Egypt had their bands with them.

Before the expedition set out, Bonaparte specifically instructed Desaix to complete the bands of each of his units and even specified that he should give a band to the 21st Light Demi-Brigade if it had none. Furthermore, during Desaix' campaign into upper Egypt, the band of the 61st Line Demi-Brigade which was being carried down the Nile with a shipment of wounded was captured. Its captors forced its musicians to play while they were slaughtering their compatriots and then executed every single one of them.

In February of 1793 another major change had been set in place for the infantry units. In order to provide more immediate firepower on the battlefield, each demi-brigade was allocated a battery of six 4-pounder guns. The artillery company necessary to man these was organised along the lines of the grenadier company.

In 1794, the artillery company was re-organised as follows:

# THE FRENCH ARMY OF THE ORIENT 1798–1801

An infantry band. Of the same publisher and in the same style as the infantry section, this is a very rare representation. The number of musicians is very close to regulation (8) with the drum-major in addition and the triangle held by a child (probably a regimental child pressed into serving in the band). This is probably exactly what each demi-brigade band looked like.

2 Captains
3 Lieutenants
1 Sergeant-Major
5 Sergeants
1 Quartermaster-Corporal
5 Corporals
1 Drummer
35 First Gunners
4 Explosive Experts
4 Craftsmen
32 Second Gunners
A total of 93 men.

They were uniformed just like the regular line artillery in full dark blue with scarlet piping. By mid-1795, a shortage of guns forced the number of allocated pieces to be brought down to three, or one per battalion. Finally in February of 1798, the artillery companies were disbanded to reinforce regular artillery. This was not to be the last time over the Napoleonic period that regimental artillery would be created and then suppressed.

However, infantry units which were to embark under Bonaparte's command were specifically excluded from this order. Therefore, the infantry demi-brigades which set out for Egypt went with their regimental artillery and therefore had their three light guns with them.

## The Infantry – Revised Organisation 1799-1801

For the Army of the Orient, this initial organisation, perfectly in line with the overall French army regulations, was to last until the summer of 1799. The units that had returned from Syria had lost on average 25 per cent of their men, and in the case of the infantry more than that and up to over 30 per cent in Lannes' division. This meant that battalions, which already were not at full strength, looked even worse off and were in a deplorable state as to their numbers.

An important set of measures was decided by Bonaparte on 9 Messidor Year VII (27 June 1799). It is important to note that these decisions do not seem to have been carried out immediately as some memoirs state that the decision was taken by Kléber, meaning that down to the rank and file, they actually saw this happening in the early autumn.

Two sets of orders were communicated: one purely related to the infantry organisation, the other one to add artillery to the infantry units.

In the first order, the demi-brigade structure was left at three battalions. However instead of each battalion having nine companies, it was now to consist of only five companies including one of grenadiers or carabiniers.

The grenadier and carabinier company structure was also changed to actually increase its force:

Unchanged : 1 Captain
Unchanged: 1 Lieutenant
Changed: 2 Second Lieutenants (was 1)
Unchanged: 1 Sergeant-Major
Changed: 4 Sergeants (was 2)
Unchanged: 1 Quartermaster-Corporal
Changed: 8 Corporals (was 4)
Unchanged: 2 Drummers
Changed: 70 Grenadiers (was 48)

In addition no detail is given as to the 4 chosen men previously outlined. The net increase in force was of 25 men overall. The composition of the other companies was unchanged.

At the demi-brigade level, a new type of company was however created. A company of scouts (éclaireurs). The way this company was to be organised was as follows:

From the 1st battalion: one captain, one second lieutenant, one sergeant, two corporals and four scouts per company, i.e. 20 scouts.

From the 2nd battalion: one lieutenant, one sergeant-major, one sergeant, two corporals, and again four scouts per company, i.e. 20 scouts.

From the 3rd battalion: another second-lieutenant, one sergeant, one quarter-master corporal, two corporals and four scouts per company, i.e. 20 scouts.

The scouts company therefore comprised:

1 Captain
1 Lieutenant

2 Second Lieutenants
1 Sergeant-Major
3 Sergeants
1 Quartermaster-Corporal
6 Corporals
60 Scouts
A total of 75 men.

The order specifies that this company is to be brought together only when it is to be used, i.e. on the battlefield. It also indicates it must be at full strength at all times. This means that the Adjudant NCO of the battalion had to give to the officer in charge of the scouts in that battalion every day the list of men composing them. During the roll call, the scouts were to be called out just after the corporals, in effect singling them out just like 'chosen men'. In addition, each scout was entitled to high pay of an extra five sols per decade (let us remember that the seven-day week had been replaced by the 'decade' or ten days). In effect this was creating a new elite company alongside the grenadiers/carabiniers, but whose extra pay was roughly half of the extra given to the grenadiers.

When lined up for use, the order indicates that the two sections of scouts are to be forward of the demi-brigade. The first section was to be in advance of the 1st and 2nd battalions at the level of the space which exists between them. The second section was to occupy the equivalent space ahead of the gap between the 2nd and 3rd battalions. However, if there were better tactical positions to be held, there were to occupy these, such as houses, trees etc. the scouts were to be aligned in ranks of two men deep.

Infantry scouts were not a total novelty in the French army. The origin of the light infantry came from the foot parts of the chasseur legions and they were originally scouts. In Italy and in other theatres of operations, some temporary scouts on foot were assembled and used. This, however, seems to be the first time that such a detailed and systematic organisation was put in place. We know that in 1804, six years after this, Napoleon would create voltigeur companies in each infantry regiment, which were to perform very much as per the duties set for the scout companies in 1798, with the difference that the company was to be together at all times and be posted on the left of the battalion.

No details of a specific badge or change in uniform for the scouts is given. As the composition of the scouts could change on a daily basis, this is fairly understandable.

The second order addressed specifically the regimental artillery.

- Each infantry battalion will have a 3-pounder gun, the lightest possible
- They will be drawn by four good horses or mules, ammunition will be carried by three camels.
- Each piece will have ammunition as follows: 130 balls, 130 grapeshot canisters.
- Each gun will be serviced by a picket of eight men. Two will be devoted to the transport, 6 to the actual servicing. These eight men will rotate

fortnightly. All the battalion will therefore service the gun in turn. The only men who will not perform this duty are the grenadiers and men who are judged not to be intelligent enough for this task. During this service, this picket will have a high pay of one sol per day.
- In addition, one sergeant per battalion will be devoted exclusively to the servicing of the gun. Likewise one corporal will be in charge of ammunition, transport, and supply.
- A the demi-brigade level, one officer will have the overall command of the three guns and will report directly to the chef de brigade.

In effect, this does not seem to much change the way that the regimental artillery was set up, but it actually did.

Previously the gunners were a separate company tasked only with artillery. As of the summer/autumn of 1799, the gunner companies ceased to formally exist and were replaced by regular infantrymen trained in artillery duty. The surviving skilled artillerymen were actually transferred to the line artillery following the losses incurred in Syria. This also means that the regimental guns were serviced by men dressed as regular infantry. One will also note some tactical elements:

- The guns have to be as light as possible. Given the Egyptian landscape this can easily be understood.
- The ammunition is evenly split between balls and grapeshot. The effectiveness of guns using grapeshot against Mameluke cavalry does not need to be demonstrated.
- Finally, unlike in Europe where the purpose of regimental artillery is open to debate, its use as part of the square tactic is unquestioned.

## Infantry Tactics in Egypt

The base for all infantry manoeuvres remained the famous 1791 infantry regulations. Based on all previous sets developed throughout the 18th century and much inspired by Prussian theories as put forward by Frederick the Great, they were to remain in effect for the most part into the 1830s. However, as the French army gained experience, the regulations were not modified per se but additions were brought in. One major improvement which was almost systematically added as an appendix in later editions was the 'Carré d'Égypte' – the Egyptian Square. Rectangular rather than square and formed three ranks deep, this formation was first formally documented in instructions published in 1805.

In reality, the real difference in square tactics utilised by the French in Egypt is that this formation was the one most effective against the Mamelukes and Ottomans. Egyptian and Turkish cavalry tactics were basic and simple. The cavalryman was well equipped with all kinds of weapons: pistols, blunderbuss, mace, axe, lance, and the dreaded oriental curved sabre. By combining speed and shock, the aim would be to break any formation and then attack the small dispersed groups. However by sticking to a rigid square formation, presenting three rows of bayonets combined with an effective rolling fire, the French could break any Mameluke or Turkish cavalry assault.

# THE FRENCH ARMY OF THE ORIENT 1798–1801

Lannes. Another portrait by Dutertre. It shows Lannes as a young man. One will note the very long and distinctive queue which he insisted on keeping until well into the Empire. Lannes was originally a plain infantryman and had risen through the ranks.

Furthermore, the square could be reinforced at its angles with regimental artillery adding further devastating firepower.

Present-day readers of Napoleonic history will certainly be familiar with the square vs. cavalry, especially in the battles for 1805-1815, but we tend to forget that the earlier Revolutionary period battles did not involve large masses of cavalry and little if any major charges against infantry. The square formation, although regulated, was not systematically used. Used for the first time at the first shock on 13 July at Chebreiss, it was employed again on 22 July at the Pyramids. From then on, squares become the rule. They could be formed at any relevant level: demi-brigade, brigade, division. At El Chelel on 21 May 1799, 200 men from the 21st Light Demi-Brigade formed square and fought off some 400 cavalrymen and 300 infantrymen.

When attacked by cavalry, the square remained stationary, but when advancing, the units moved in square formation. Thus at Heliopolis, Kléber advanced towards the enemy with his four brigades in square formation. Savary noted that for the Battle of the Pyramids, the infantry marched in square for nineteen hours! Such long marching spells in such a formation were extremely trying as the men would be in very close order, whilst their steps would raise massive clouds of dust which would choke them. Add to this the heat of Egypt and one cannot but admire the tenacity of the French infantry faced with such hardship. As soon as possible, the units would revert to a column formation. But if ever enemy cavalry was expected, the units were put back in square, even for a bivouac!

Given the success of the square formation, Bonaparte considered further reinforcing it by having each infantryman carry a 1.60m pole with a metal spike at both ends. When forming the square, each soldier would plant his spike just ahead of him and it would be tied to its immediate neighbouring spike thanks to a small metal chain. This anti-cavalry palisade could be formed three ranks deep and should have ensured the charging Mamelukes would first fall on this dangerous barrier. This decision was set forth in a daily order on 21 January 1799 and poles were manufactured by the artillery in time for the Syrian expedition. However the heat of the Syrian desert and the weight of the pole put a quick stop to this experiment and poles were quickly discarded by the troops on their way to El Arich.

The first employment of the square formation against the Mamelukes had also shown that the tactics spelled out in the 1791 regulation could be improved. Having the first rank with a knee on the ground made it very vulnerable to Mameluke attacks. Likewise the method of having the ranks pass their muskets backwards for reloading mean that during that time the soldiers could be hit by the enemy cavalry. Consequently, also in January 1799, the French infantry was ordered to stay on three ranks, but all standing.

The third rank would fire first, then, while it was reloading, the two first ranks would discharge their weapons.

Finally, outside of the battlefield, the ferocious guerrilla nature of the fighting forced the French to arm themselves adequately. A general order ensured that officers and drummers would carry a short musket as early as September of 1798. This measure was extended to other men from other branches. In effect, almost no French soldier could take to the field without having some significant firepower, ensuring both his own defence but also providing incremental firepower on the battlefield.

Finally there were only two major occasions when the French infantry went back to the more traditional European modes of manoeuvring, line and column. The first time was at the land battle of Aboukir where the lack of discipline on the Turkish side ensured its defeat. The second time was at Alexandria/Canope facing the British. Obviously, on the latter occasion, the lack of training in performing such complex movements in the dark by troops who bore little resemblance to those who had landed in 1798, ensured defeat this time for the French side.

## Infantry Unit Histories

2nd Light Demi-Brigade: initially part of Kléber's division, it fought under Dugua at the Pyramids and during the rebellion in Cairo. Kléber again commanded it as part of his division for the Syrian campaign. Its main act of glory was at the battle of Nazareth on 8 April 1799 where 150 of its carabiniers fought under Junot. Subsequently, they were awarded a sabre for this action. Its commander, Desnoyer was killed in November 1799, much to Kléber's dismay. Subsequently the 2nd Light mutinied and Kléber had to disband it. Following disciplinary actions and enquiries, he reformed the unit but without the elite carabinier companies.

Chefs de Brigade:

Desnoyers: up to November 1799, killed in action at Damiette

Schramm: chef de battalion, acting chef de brigade, confirmed only in November 1801.

4th Light Demi-Brigade: part of Bon's division at the Pyramids. Only the 1st battalion went into Syria where it fought at Mount-Thabor. Back in Egypt the full demi-brigade fights at Aboukir, Heliopolis and Alexandria/Canope.

Chefs de Brigade:

Destaing: Promoted to général de brigade on the field of battle at the Pyramids, 21 July 1798.

Lacroix, formerly chef de battalion, promoted to acting chef de brigade as of July 1798

Bazancourt: promoted to chef de brigade by Menou 27 April 1801

7th Light Demi-Brigade: Only the 3rd battalion was part of the Army of the Orient. It was used for service on board the ships of the fleet and was afterwards left in Malta as part of Vaubois' force.

# THE FRENCH ARMY OF THE ORIENT 1798–1801

Junot, like Lannes, had come from the infantry ranks. He was brave to the point of being reckless. This interesting portrait by Dutertre actually even shows a large scar on the right temple. Plagued by numerous head wounds, he eventually became insane and had to be removed from command in 1812.

**21st Light Demi-Brigade:** One of the most famous of Egyptian units, part of Desaix' division. It fought at the Pyramids and then went deep into Upper-Egypt where it fought at Sediman giving its commander Robin the rank of général de brigade. It fought at Aboukir, Heliopolis and lastly at Alexandria/Canope. It was probably the unit which was the most reinforced with non-French soldiers: Darfur slaves, Copts etc.

Chefs de Brigade:

Robin: As indicated above promoted to général de brigade at Sediman

Eppler: Was promoted to chef de brigade after Robin. He was wounded at Canope/Alexandria in March 1801 and promoted to général de brigade 27 April 1801.

Tarayre: Promoted to chef de brigade in replacement of Eppler.

**22nd Light Demi-Brigade:** Part of Lannes' division, fought at Alexandria, the Pyramids. In the Syrian campaign it fought at Gaza, Jaffa (where its commander Lejeune is killed). Was at Acre and then Aboukir and Heliopolis.

Chefs de Brigade:

Chavardés: badly wounded at the storming of Alexandria and shipped back to France for health reasons

Lejeune: replaces Chavardés; killed at the siege of Jaffa

Goguet: promoted chef de brigade 9 October 1799

**9th Line Demi-Brigade:** Part of Reynier's division. It was part of the assault on Malta and then at Chebreiss and the Pyramids. It participated in the Syrian campaign (Acre) and was at Heliopolis. Part of the Cairo garrison in 1800. This is one of the best known units thanks to its well-known commander Pepin and the fact that his orderly book had survived and was partially published at the end of the 19th century in 'La Sabretache'.

Chefs de Brigade:

Marpaude: leaves very quickly to go back to France for health reasons (he was 43 years old).

Pepin: acting chef de brigade (confirmed under the Consulate).

**13th Line Demi-Brigade:** Part of Lannes' division, participated in the assault on Malta and was at the Pyramids. Only the 1st and 2nd battalions go to Syria: the 3rd battalion is left in Egypt as part of the garrison forces. Greatly distinguished at Heliopolis.

Chefs de Brigade:

Delegorgue: promoted to général de brigade on the field of battle at Heliopolis, 20 March 1800

# DOING MUCH WITH LITTLE: ORGANISATION AND TACTICS

Froment: replaces Delegorgue on 25 April 1800

18th Line Demi-Brigade: Part of Bon's division (was Menou's) it was at Chebreiss and during the Cairo insurrection was charged with taking over the main Cairo fortress. The 1st and 2nd battalions are in Syria: again, the 3rd battalion is left as a garrison force in Egypt. At Acre, in the assault of 7 May 1799, Chef de Brigade Boyer is killed and there are 23 officers casualties. Again at the forefront of the assault at Aboukir, led by General Fugière who is gravely wounded. Finally at Alexandria/Canope where it was badly mauled leaving only 308 men return to France.

Chefs de Brigade:
Boyer: killed at the siege of Acre
Morangiés: promoted to chef de brigade on 13 May 1799, and then to général de brigade on 24 May 1801; badly wounded at Canope/Alexandria.
Ravier: promoted to chef de brigade on 27 April 1801

19th Line Demi-Brigade: Part of the Malta assault and then its two battalions stay on as part of Vaubois' occupation force. Its grenadiers, however, follow on to Egypt as troops attached to the general headquarters. Over time, these men are dispersed across other units.

25th Line Demi-Brigade: Part of Dugua's division present at Alexandria, Chebreiss and the Pyramids. The first two battalions formed part of Kléber's division for the Syrian campaign and were at Mount-Thabor and Acre. On 10 May 1799 Chef de Brigade Venoux leading the assault with his grenadiers, is killed.

Chefs de Brigade:
Venoux: killed at the siege of Acre
Lefebvre: promoted to chef de brigade on 19 June 1799, then to général de brigade under Menou on 29 May 1801
Cassagne: promoted to chef de brigade on 29 May 1801

32nd Line Demi-Brigade: Bon's division, present at the Pyramids, Mount-Thabor and Acre. Chef de Brigade d'Armagnac is promoted to général de brigade his bravery at Acre.

Chefs de Brigade:
Dupuy: promoted on the field of battle at the Pyramids to général de brigade; subsequently commander of Cairo, killed during the first rebellion
Darmagnac: promoted to chef de brigade in replacement of Dupuy on 26 July 1798.
Darricau: promoted to chef de brigade on 13 March 1801

41st Line Demi-Brigade: Initially charged with fleet service, the men of the 41st are left in Malta as part of Vaubois' division.

61st Line Demi-Brigade: Part of Desaix' division. Fought at Cheresis, the Pyramids, Sediman, in Upper-Egypt, and then the Aboukir land battle. Ironically, the 61st had also been present at the Aboukir sea battle (or

Battle of the Nile) as Desaix had left a detachment on board the ship *Timoleon*.

Chefs de Brigade:
Conroux: killed during the siege of Cairo, second rebellion
Dorsenne: promoted to chef de brigade May 1800

69th Line Demi-Brigade: Initially part of Menou's division, it is the one infantry unit which is left behind in Alexandria. Later the two first battalions join Lannes' division for the Syrian campaign while the 3rd is left behind as part of the Cairo garrison. Its chef de brigade, Barthelemy is killed at Zeitah. Back in Egypt it takes a major part in the Battle of Aboukir and the battle honour is put on its flag. It comes back to France having lost two-thirds of its strength.

Chefs de Brigade:
Barthélémy: killed 15 March 1799
Eyssautier: died of plague in Alexandria
Brun: promoted to chef de brigade on 3 June 1800

75th Line Demi-Brigade: Part of Dugua's division, fought at the Pyramids. Its 1st and 2nd battalion went Syria as part of Kléber's division, fighting at Mount Thabor and Acre.. At Canope/Alexandria its flag is saved by Lieutenant Volland.

Chefs de Brigade:
Maugras: promoted to général de brigade in September 1800, dies of fever in Damiette in 1801
L'Huillier: promoted to chef de brigade September 1800

79th Line Demi-Brigade: formally part of the Army of the Orient but actually part of the Corfu garrison under General Chabot.

80th Line Demi-Brigade: Part of Vaubois' Malta garrison, one battalion and three grenadier companies.

85th Line Demi-Brigade: Part of Reynier's division. Fought at Chebreiss and the Pyramids. Its first two battalions are part of the Syrian expedition. At Canope/Alexandria, Drummer Dache is awarded drumsticks of honour.

Chefs de Brigade:
Eberlé: returns to France in late 1798 due to bad health.
Davroux: replaces Eberlé and is killed at the siege of Acre
Viala: promoted to chef de brigade on 19 May 1799

88th Line Demi-Brigade: Part of Desaix' division. Fought at the Pyramids and in Upper-Egypt. It suffers major losses at Sediman where 20 men of the demi-brigade fought off 300 enemies. At the end, only five men are left. Fusilier Guéry commanding them is saved by a grenadier company. It has 'Sediman' as a battle honour on its flag.

Chefs de Brigade:
Silly: promoted to général de brigade, 23 September 1800

Curial: promoted in replacement of Silly the same day; both were severely wounded at Alexandria/Canope.

## The Cavalry: Organisation and Tactics

Under the royalty the cavalry and the navy had been the darling branches of military service for the nobility. When the Revolutionary troubles hit their peak, some of the cavalry regiments simply emigrated as a full unit. All units felt the impact on morale and efficiency as good officers, and sometimes men, would join the counter-Revolutionary armies. Yet, just like for the infantry, there was no lack of enthusiasm in the French population and volunteer units sprang up across the countries. Some of the names are well known: 'Hussars of Death', sometimes almost comical 'Poacher-Hussars'. The nature of the fighting quickly showed that more light cavalry was need for scouting and generally speaking 'la petite guerre'. To this effect, volunteer units were merged with regular units, dragoons were to be considered light cavalry, and the number of squadrons per regiment was raised to six.. However, the tough reality of recruitment and training resulted in going back to more reasonable numbers.

Another oddity is that, although the commanding officer was named chef de brigade, the unit he commanded was still called a regiment.

The cavalerie regiments, which were considered heavy cavalry along with the two carabinier regiments and which were in time to form the future cuirassiers, campaigned only the northern and German theatres of war. Dragoons, hussars and chasseurs formed the cavalry that Bonaparte had with him in Italy, and this was to be again the case for Egypt. As can be seen in the detailed orders of battle, only 2,800 cavalrymen were taken along with barely 700 horses. In the planning done in early 1798, Bonaparte had assumed some 10-12,000 horses could be easily found in Egypt. Needless to say this fact never materialised! Fortunately, slightly more than two-thirds of the cavalry was composed of dragoons who were also trained to fight on foot and carried a musket which was shorter than the regular infantry model. By mid-August, the cavalry had at its disposal close to 850 mounts, which seems just barely more than the initial 700. Actually, all the French horses had been assigned to the artillery, and these were fresh Arab horses which the French cavalry would from then on use. However, although a cavalry depot and remount service was set up in Boulaq near Cairo, mounted strength never came any close to what had been planned back in Paris.

According to the decree of 16 January 1797, each 'ight cavalry regiment was to be formed of four squadrons, each having two companies. Each company was organised as:

1 Captain
1 Lieutenant
2 Junior Lieutenants
1 First Sergeant
4 Sergeants
1 Farrier corporal
8 Corporals

# THE FRENCH ARMY OF THE ORIENT 1798–1801

Lasalle, for a month or so just after the start of the campaign, was a dragoon officer – this is when Dutertre sketched him. This is both fortunate, as we have a wonderful portrait of the young Lasalle with a typical fancy dragoon officer helmet, and unfortunate, as it seems Dutertre did not draw any of the hussar or chasseur officers.

1 Trumpeter
1 Blacksmith
95 Troopers
This totalled 115 men.

Note that, by tradition in France, the rank of sergeant (sergent) and corporal (caporal) bore a different name in the cavalry and gendarmerie. A sergeant of mounted troops was called a 'maréchal des logis' (plural: maréchaux des logis) and a corporal, a brigadier. The last must of course not confused with the English rank of that name which was the equivalent of général de brigade!

The regimental staff stood as follows

1 Chef de Brigade
2 Chefs d'Escadrons (chiefs of squadron; having actually two squadrons to command each)
1 Quartermaster Treasurer
1 Senior Surgeon
1 Junior Surgeon
2 Adjutant NCOs
1 Veterinarian
1 Master Saddler
1 Master Armorer & Spur-maker
1 Master Tailor
1 Master Cobbler
This gave a total of 13.

In total and on paper, each regiment would therefore align a little over 900 men.

Although some of best of the empire's future cavalry leaders fought in Egypt – Lasalle, Colbert and of course Murat – French cavalry was not on par with that of the Mamelukes when it came to fighting. Open mêlées showed very quickly that the sabres used by French cavalry did not match the quality of those used by the Mamelukes, who in addition but were far more heavily armed. As a consequence, all officers were asked to carry a short shoulder firearm of some kind. Many adopted local blunderbusses. Also, sabres were quick to be exchanged with Mameluke weapons seized on the field of battle. Likewise, French saddles were often discarded in favour of local saddles and stirrups. The main role of the cavalry ended up being what it knew best, scouting, and that required it to be equipped for local conditions. Daure's correspondence frequently mentions the need to supply cavalry units with coats, blankets and, even more importantly, water containers. Each cavalryman seems to have set out loaded with at least two large leather containers to ensure the necessary supply and possible replenishment when arriving at a water source. French cavalry ultimately had to adapt from its own culture of dashing bravery to more pragmatic attitudes and tactics.

In the following (well-known) description by Desvernois of his first encounter and duel with a Mameluke at the Battle of the Pyramids, his attitude is typical of the brave French hussar officer:

> As the battle was coming to its end, a giant Mameluke Bey with a long beautiful white beard jumped out from the entrenchments of Embabeh and paraded along the front of General Bon's division, shooting his pistols, provoking the French troops. I am struck with anger at the sight of this impudent enemy, and, spurring my superb Arab steed into gallop, I dash though Bon's square at lightning speed to get to this daring Bey. Cannon balls fly around us, but we do not care for them. With one pistol shot I throw my adversary to the ground. He manages to break loose from his mount and crawls on his hands and knees to come closer to me. Seeing him, with his white beard, scrapping the ground right to left with his sabre, I understand he is making a plea for mercy, and in order for him to understand that I wish him not harm, I put my sabre under my left elbow, its point to my back, the pommel to the front and I extend my arms open. But I had misunderstood him, he continues with his sabre; cautious I move sideways my horse so its legs are not hurt. This slight movement gives an edge to my enemy. He is covered by my horse's neck and springs up like a snake grabbing my stirrups with his left hand while striking at me with his sabre in his right hand with all his might … But my horse receives the blow, by a sharp move it had jumped and it had struck the bridge of its nose. Like lightning I strike back at my enemy two strong blows to the arm and hand which has seized the stirrups and two or three to his head and other arm. Seriously wounded but not disarmed, the Bey kneels once more and again repeats his little game. But I've played long enough and bowing down on to him, I break open his skull.

In 1835, in the *Journal de l'Armée*, one of the many periodicals then being published for the military, the following article was inserted.

> More than once, General Bonaparte has his life saved thanks to the firepower of his escort, formed as a battle line or even in square against a superior Mameluke force which only this type of tactic could hold off. At Salahieh, the 7th Hussars under the command of squadron commander d'Estrées and the 22nd Chasseurs charged the famous Mecca caravan; the 4,000 mamelukes who were protecting this convoy immediately surrounded both regiments and did great harm to them, and then came about charging the 3rd, 14th and 15th Dragoons with which Napoleon was, far away from his infantry. The general-in-chief turned to General Leclerc d'Ostein and asked 'what are you going to do?' 'Place yourself in the centre' answered Leclerc, 'officers and NCOs in the ranks, form the square we will fight like infantry'. The Mamelukes were pushed back thanks to fire by files and having rallied the 7th Hussars and 22nd Chasseurs, we walked very slowly in line of battle to the enemy carrying the muskets high. After this, a daily order stipulated a new order for cavalry when in battle, officers and NCOs were to be in the ranks rather than at the front or at the rear, exposed to enemy attacks. General Bonaparte after the storming of El-Arych moving the army towards Gaza found himself alone with an escort of 150 Guides at Kayounes on the eastern side of the Egyptian border. Instead of finding Kléber's division which they were expecting

# THE FRENCH ARMY OF THE ORIENT 1798–1801

Boussart, chef de brigade of the 20th Dragoons. It is interesting to compare his helmet as with Lasalle's: one can really see that many variations existed, especially amongst officers, even though the overall shape and style remained the same.

there, and which had lost its way in the desert, stumbled upon Ibrahim-Bey's Mamelukes which numbered some 2 to 3,000. As they could not retreat safely, they gambled with audacity and decided to form a square to stop the movement of the enemy and wait either for the division or for nightfall which would allow them to escape. At Gaza, again without his infantry, Bonaparte had to draw his sword and order that the entire cavalry form a line of battle and wait, muskets high, to push back the Turkish charge. On the road from Jaffa to Acre, the cavalry again met alone Ibrahim-Bey and his Mamelukes and again stood its ground thanks to musketry.

When drafting the Year XIII cavalry regulations, the Prince of Neufchâtel (Berthier) asked one of the authors, Colonel Curto to include the cavalry square. The colonel, who had been present in the four encounters aforementioned, despite this was opposed to doing so. Irritated, Napoleon paid him a visit at the break of dawn and asked him abruptly 'what is the strength of cavalry', 'in its impulse, Sire'. A nod from the Emperor and the approval from all other witnesses present, showed the answer was the right one and this great captain who had first found extraordinary that a mere colonel might defy him in terms of tactics, no longer mentioned defensive positions for cavalry when on its own.

Indeed, given the conditions of European warfare and the much improved quality of French cavalry, Curto's answer was the right one. However, the lessons learned in Egypt had to be repeated in the 1830s for the benefit of the younger generation of French military who were then fighting a similar war in Algeria.

But, it is worthy to note that the French cavalry did make one final massive charge at Alexandria/Canope. This was against the will of its commander, General Roize, who knew this was to prove fatal to his men. Roize did obey and like so many of his dragoons was killed during the action.

## Cavalry Unit Histories

3rd Dragoons: formerly the 'Régiment de Bourbon', it had fought in Italy and was present at the Pyramids, Syria (Nazareth and Mount Thabor), Aboukir, and Alexandria/Canope.
Chefs de Brigade:
Bron de Bailly: promoted to général de brigade in September 1800 by Menou
Fiteau: promoted to chef de brigade in September 1800

14th Dragoons: formerly 'Régiment de Chartres', in Italy as of 1798. Fought at the Pyramids, then in Upper-Egypt under Davout and then in Syria with Murat, fighting at Nazareth. At Aboukir, its chef de brigade, Duvivier, is killed.
Chefs de Brigade:
Duvivier: killed at Aboukir
Lambert: promoted to chef de brigade to replace Duvivier in 1799
Lafond Blaniac: promoted to chef de brigade in April 1801

# DOING MUCH WITH LITTLE: ORGANISATION AND TACTICS

15th Dragoons: formerly 'Régiment de Noailles'. It was in Italy 1796-1798. Fought at Chebreiss, the Pyramids and then in Upper-Egypt. Part of the regiment was in the Syrian campaign. It also distinguished itself at Heliopolis.
Chefs de Brigade:
Pinon: killed in Upper-Egypt
Barthelemy: promoted to chef de brigade 21 June 1799

18th Dragoons: formerly 'Régiment du Roi'. In Italy 1796-1798, where it distinguished itself at Rivoli. Present at the Pyramids, in Upper-Egypy, and Syria.
Chefs de Brigade:
Ledée: remained all throughout the expedition

20th Dragoons: Unlike the other units, this was not a former royal regiment but one raised from a volunteer unit the 'Dragons de Jemappes'. In 1797-1798 it was in Italy. It was the only cavalry unit to participate in the storming of Alexandria. It was then charged with moving ahead Desaix' division during the march towards Cairo, becoming the first unit to encounter Mamelukes at Chebreiss. Fought at the Pyramids, in the Syrian campaign, and then at Aboukir, Heliopolis etc. For bravery during the Battle of the Pyramids, it was awarded that battle honour to bear on its guidon.
Chefs de Brigade:
Boussart: promoted to général de brigade, 23 September 1800
Reynaud: promoted to chef de brigade in September 1800

22nd Chasseurs: Another recent unit, raised from the 'Légion des Pyrénées Orientales' (Legion of the Eastern Pyrenees). It was in Italy 1796-1798. Its commander in Egypt is Lasalle who was to rise to immortal fame during the Empire as the ultimate light cavalry leader. It is at Salahieh (see above), but then in Upper-Egypt. One squadron went to Syria and the full unit then fought at Aboukir and Heliopolis.
Chefs de Brigade:
Lasalle: left for France in mid-1800
Latour-Maubourg: arrived in Egypt in 1800 and replaced Lasalle on 22 July 1800.

7th *bis* Hussars: This was the second 'seventh' regiment of hussars to be raised, hence its '*bis*' numbering equivalent to '7b' in French! Originally raised as the 'Hussards de la Liberté' (Liberty Hussars), a volunteer unit, it had transferred to the Army of Italy in 1795. It fought at Chebreiss and the Pyramids and then fought mainly in Upper-Egypt. It was at Aboukir and Heliopolis. In 1802, this regiment was transformed (much to the fury of its men) into the 28th Dragoons.
Chefs de Brigade:
Duplessis: killed in Upper-Egypt
Detrès: promoted to chef de brigade on 14 August 1798 to replace Duplessis

## Artillery

Three artillery regiments provided troops to the expedition, the 3rd, 4th, 5th and 8th Light Artillery (mounted or horse artillery) and the 1st, 4th and 6th Foot Artillery Regiments Actually, however, this information has no real importance. By that stage, in the artillery, the regimental organisation was only for administrative purposes. A full artillery regiment never took to the field as a unit. Tactically, the individual company was the equivalent of a battery and operated independently. As such, the Army of the Orient was comprised of 14 foot artillery companies and four horse artillery companies.

The horse artillery was a very recent innovation in the French army and dated back only to the first years of the French Revolution. Initially called 'flying artillery', it had been born of the need to provide mobile fire support on the battlefield. Its start, during the first years of the Revolution had been somewhat chaotic. Its men had to be both artillerymen and good horse riders.

As indicated, one company equated to one battery, both for foot and horse. The composition of a foot artillery company was:

2 Captains (one 1st class, one 2nd class)
1 First Lieutenant
2 Second Lieutenants
1 Sergeant-Major
1 Farrier Corporal
1 Drummer
5 Sergeants
5 Corporals
35 Gunners, 1st class
40 Gunners, 2nd class
In total: 93 men

As for a horse artillery company:

1 Captain (either 1st or 2nd class)
1 First Lieutenant
2 Second Lieutenants
1 Sergeant-Major ('chef')
4 Sergeants (maréchaux des logis)
1 Farrier Corporal
4 Corporals (brigadiers)
2 Trumpeters
30 Gunners, 1st class
30 Gunners, 2nd class
Total: 76 men

In addition to the regular artillery companies, two companies of 'artillery workers' (ouvriers) was also sent to the expedition. Such a company fielded 4 officers (1 captain, 1 first lieutenant, 2 second lieutenants) and 83 men of which 40 were workers and 30 'apprentices'.

The two pontoon battalions were considered part of the artillery. Each battalion had 8 companies. One of those companies was sent to Egypt. The organisation of such a company was:

1 Captain (1st or 2nd class)
1 Lieutenant (1st or 2nd class)
1 Sergeant-Major
2 Sergeants
1 Farrier Corporal
4 Corporals
7 Workers
1 Drummer
56 Pontonniers
Total: 78 men

As odd as it may seem, the artillery train was not a military branch of service. The transport of artillery equipment was supported by private companies. This was no exception for Egypt, however, it was decided that the men (drivers) would be under the direct responsibility and command of artillery officers. In effect, the train had become militarised, although it was still a private service. This was absolutely necessary in Egypt given the distance from France and it proved a successful change. The lesson was learnt and both artillery and supply trains became military branches of service under the Consulate and the Empire. In Egypt, the train was organised by company with NCOs coming from the army:

1 Sergeant-major
2 Sergeants
4 Corporals
1 Blacksmith
1 Harness maker
40 Drivers 1st class
20 Drivers 2nd class
Total: 69 men

As can be seen from the various orders of battle, the equipment used by the artillery of the army was far from being homogeneous. Many guns had been captured from the Austrians or Piedmontese. As the campaign dragged on, the artillery workers as well as engineers were pressed into providing much needed repairs or even casting guns and building carriages. Turkish and British guns were also captured, so by 1801, the park was quite diversified.

Some attempt was made to use camels to draw guns. In the famous *Description de l'Égypte* plates one can indeed see this. However, other testimonials tend to say this was not that effective. As much as possible, artillery was drawn by horses or mules.

## Engineers

There were no engineer regiments or demi-brigades, but only battalions. As of January 1798, the French army was to field four sapper battalions each composed of eight companies, each company being of 200 men in total.

    1 Captain (1st or 2nd class)
    2 Lieutenants (one 1st class, one 2nd class)
    1 Sergeant-Major
    1 Farrier Corporal
    1 Iron Craftsman
    1 Wood Craftsman
    1 Drummer
    4 Sergeants
    8 Corporals
    180 Sappers
    Total: 200 men

Two balloon companies were part of the engineers. These were officially disbanded on 17 February 1799. However, the first balloon company was in Egypt and therefore continued to exist. As we have seen elsewhere, as it had lost all of its ballooning equipment with the sinking of the *Orient* at the Battle of the Nile, it did not serve really as a balloon corps. Conté, who was its commanding officer, provided with his men and other craftsmen a wider range of tasks. The company was organised as follows:

    1 Captain
    1 Lieutenant
    1 Sergeant-Major
    1 Sergeant
    2 Corporals
    20 Men
    Total: 26 men.

The French did fly at least one balloon to celebrate the anniversary of the Republic in September 1798. Although much is made of this event in French memoirs and contemporary texts, it did not seem to have impressed the locals that much. Sheikh Al Jabarti commented ironically in his diary that this was no better than the kites Egyptians children would fly!

## Logistical Train

The logistical train (train des équipages) was much less militarised than the artillery train. In Egypt it was very much under the responsibility of the war commissary. Much of the transport was carried out using donkeys, mules, and camels. Camels became an essential part of the army logistics and this comes up regularly in the daily orders and war commissary correspondence.

## Units Raised for the Army of the Orient

For this section, the units are described in their chronological order of creation.

### The Guides

Army commanders had for long realised they needed some form of personal unit to help them out on the battlefield. The Maréchal de Saxe had such a unit during the War of the Austrian Succession, and, as the Revolutionary Wars started, all army commanders soon formed their own light cavalry units attached to their staff. The generic term chosen to designate these men is guide. Indeed these cavalrymen were supposed to be intelligent and resourceful so that they could go on scouting missions and deliver messages, but also act as bodyguards for their general.

In Italy, Bonaparte had raised such a unit known as the Guides de l'Armée d'Italie under the command of Captain Bessières. Far from staying a pure cavalry unit, it became over time a miniature army corps comprised of cavalry, infantry, and artillery. In essence, the guides were very much the ancestors of the future Consular and Imperial Guard. By 1798, Bessières had risen to the rank of chef de brigade and had under him some 700 men. It is that unit which was to cross over into Egypt, adopting the name of Guides de l'Armée d'Orient.

On 19 June 1798, while still on board the *Orient*, Bonaparte decided on the organisation of the Guides as being seven companies (four mounted, three on foot) and three auxiliary companies (one mounted, two on foot).

Caffarelli, probably one of the best known officers in Egypt. Caffarelli was a true soldier-scientist and his death a huge loss to the army as he was also a superb organiser. His brother was also a distinguished officer who led a prosperous career in the Consular and then Imperial Guard.

Staff:
- 1 Chef de Brigade
- 3 Chefs d'Escadron
- 1 Treasurer Quartermaster
- 2 First Lieutenants, Adjutants
- 2 Second Lieutenants, Adjutants
- 1 Medical Officer
- 1 Trumpet-Major
- 1 Trumpet-Corporal
- 1 Drum-Major
- 1 Veterinary Officer
- 1 Master Boot-maker
- 1 Master Saddler
- 1 Master Cobbler
- 1 Master Tailor
- 1 Master Armourer
- 20 Mounted Musicians

Total staff: 39

Mounted company:
- 1 Captain
- 1 First Lieutenant
- 2 Second Lieutenants
- 1 Sergeant-Major
- 4 Sergeants
- 1 Farrier-Corporal
- 4 Corporals
- 2 Trumpeters
- 100 Guides
- Total per mounted company: 116 men

Each squadron was composed of 2 companies: 232
Total mounted guides: 464

Foot company:
- 1 Captain
- 1 First Lieutenant
- 1 Second Lieutenant
- 1 Sergeant-Major
- 4 Sergeants
- 1 Farrier-Corporal
- 4 Corporals
- 2 Drummers
- 100 Guides
- Total per foot company: 115
- Total foot guides: 345

Half-company of light artillery
- 1 Captain
- 1 Lieutenant
- 1 Sergeant-Major
- 2 Sergeants
- 1 Farrier-Corporal
- 4 Corporals
- 1 Trumpeter
- 60 Mounted Gunners
- Total guide artillery: 71
- Total guides without auxiliary companies: 687

To these, one mounted and two foot auxiliary companies were to be added representing a further 346 men, so a theoretical total of 1,033 men.

In reality on 1 January 1799, only 294 mounted guides and 268 foot guides were accounted for, so a total of 562, close to the amount planned without the auxiliary companies. The auxiliary companies were to be drafted from the other army units. It is therefore logical to consider that, even if they may have existed at some stage, they had vanished within the few first months of the expedition.

As for the artillery, only 23 guide artillerymen had boarded their ship when leaving for Egypt. To ensure the guide artillery was complete, 45 gunners from the 5th Artillery were transferred to the Guides.

Upon his departure for France, according to a letter from Bessières to the Ministry of War after their landing in France, Bonaparte took with him about 100 mounted and 100 foot guides along with their commander Bessières. Chef de Battalion Deriot was named by Kléber as the new chef de brigade of the Guides. At the end of 1801, only 190 foot guides and 90 mounted guides come back to France. All the able men joined the new Consular Guard.

On 1 September 1798, Bonaparte issued an order creating a company of native foot guides and gives it command to the 'Janissary Omar', giving him the rank of captain in the French army. In the subsequent order issued by Berthier, Omar is mentioned as having given continued signs of allegiance to the French Republic and proven his courage and valour. The company was to be organised exactly along the lines of a regular guide foot company, enjoying the same pay. It was provided with a French farrier-corporal. The company was probably created, or at least partially so, but did it survive the first Cairo insurrection? One does not find any details in the various battle orders of a specific native guide company, and certainly not in early 1799.

The Maltese Legion (*Légion Maltaise*)

As we have seen, the former troops of the Knights of Malta were inspected and some then reorganised and left in Malta. The better part of them, some 1,500 men, sailed with the Army of the Orient to Egypt.

Just after the landing in Alexandria, Bonaparte ordered to Général de Division Dumuy to set up a Maltese Battalion. This unit was also given two 3-pounder guns, a French artillery officer, a war commissary, and an engineer officer as well as a French grenadier company and 25 engineer sappers. These troops were to act as a mobile column to ensure that the lines of communication between the main body of the army and Alexandria were kept open.

After this first use of Maltese troops, they were concentrated in Rahmanie where they were organised at the end of July into two battalions of 750 men each with 9 companies apiece including a grenadier company. As no trace of the original organisation decree has been found, we have to assume it followed French infantry standard organisation. This assumption is further reinforced by the fact the Maltese troops were given the same pay as French troops. On 29 August 1798, Irish-born Chef de Battalion Bernard MacSheehy was named as their commander.

The Maltese Legion also recruited Turks and Italians almost form the start. As a force, it was never very effective and the last mention of its operations is its presence at the siege of El Arish at the beginning of the Syrian campaign. It was afterwards sent back to Cairo. Daily orders often mention Maltese deserters, so it is no surprise that on 14 July 1799, the Legion was disbanded. The Maltese soldiers were transferred to all the various French units with no better success as they continued to desert!

The Nautical Legion *(Légion Nautique)*

After the disaster in Aboukir Bay (Battle of the Nile), there were quite a few unemployed seamen. Not only were there survivors, but the British had also sent back the prisoners, as, in any case, they did not seem of much harm given that all their ships were lost. On 15 August 1798, the Nautical Legion was created. It was put under the command of Capitaine de Frégate Martinet.

Kléber, who was in command of Alexandria and its surrounding area, took care of all the available sailors and detailed in a letter dated 21 August 1798 how he was using them:

- 360 have been sent to the 69th Line Demi-Brigade
- 200 navy gunners have been transferred to the artillery
- 200 seamen are now part of the Nile flotilla
- 600 have been sent to the Nautical Legion.

Thanks to another letter from Kléber to Bonaparte we know that the Nautical Legion was then organised as follows:

- 4 fusilier companies
- 1 gunner company
- 1 sapper company

By 4 November 1798, it had grown to a full nine companies, including one of grenadiers, plus the previous gunner and sapper sections. The strength was around 2,500 men.

If using these men made sense, singling them out in one unit did not turn out to be such a good idea. The army blamed the navy for being stranded in Egypt and this did not help the relationship between the Nautical Legion and the rest of the troops. Its morale was low, and its discipline suffered from all this. Just like the Maltese Legion, it was disbanded on 14 July 1799 and its men transferred to various units.

This was the end of the first Nautical Legion. While negotiating the possible return of the troops to France, Kléber asked on 9 November 1799 that all former seamen in the army be identified. After the Battle of Heliopolis, conscious that his ground forces needed to be reorganised, he went back to his idea of 1798 and re-created the Nautical Legion as of 19 April 1800. These men were used to man forts and batteries. This did not seem a bigger success. Seamen were again used in the various army units. The last trace of an organised battalion of seamen is during the siege of Alexandria in 1801 under Chef de Brigade Massé with a strength of 524 men.

The Greek Legion (*Légion Grecque*)
It became quickly obvious to the French that local Christian communities would be natural allies. On 27 September 1798, three companies of one hundred men and three officers each were organised in Cairo. They served as an escort to the Nile flotilla. Their commanding officer, Nicolas Papas-Oglou distinguished himself at their head and was finally rewarded with the command of a full-blown Greek Legion on 17 April 1800 after Heliopolis.

The legion was composed of 8 companies, including one of artillery, and by 23 September 1800 had a strength of 670 men. Its discipline and training were far from being adequate so it was reinforced with French officers. Two companies (grenadiers and scouts) fought at the Battle of Alexandria and then participated in the siege.

All the remaining men sailed back to France where they would again fight under Papas-Oglou in a new unit, the Chasseurs d'Orient which would continue into the Empire.

The Dromedaries (*Les Dromadaires*)
This unit is, by far, the most well-known and iconic of the French army in Egypt. Considered the ancestor of the future 'Meharistes' (Sahara camel corps) and to some degree that of all the future cavalry of the Army of Africa, the Dromadaires combined exoticism with a brilliant hussar-style uniform.

Bernoyer, in one of his letters to his wife, mentions that in September 1799, he was asked by Bonaparte to design the uniform for a corps of camel-mounted couriers that the latter was thinking of setting up. This project did not however come to fruition. So, the dromedaries were not organised in the first weeks or months of the expedition, but actually only in January 1799, prior to the Syrian campaign.

Bonaparte had by that point had the time to judge the transport, speed, and overall usefulness of camels in the specific climate and geography of the Middle East. He also knew that, going into Syria, he would need a mobile scouting force which would be more effective than the traditional cavalry he had. Legend says he was convinced of creating the unit after having ordered his stepson Eugene and another officer race on camel-back during a famous expedition to Suez in the very last days of 1798. It is more likely that he had been planning for this for quite some time.

On the 9 January 1799, the Régiment de Dromadaires was created composed of two squadrons, having four companies each and the companies organised as follows:

1 Captain
1 Lieutenant
1 Sergeant-Major
2 Sergeants
1 Farrier-Corporal
4 Corporals
1 Trumpeter
50 Dromedaries

Total: 61 men. In addition there was a small staff of about ten men. So the theoretical strength of the unit was roughly 500 men. All the men including the commanding officer Chef de Brigade Cavalier (ironically meaning 'cavalryman' in French) came from infantry units.

In fact the dromedaries were used to scout and when fighting would dismount and fight like infantry, sheltering behind their camels. They were without doubt the most successful unit created in Egypt. They were present and fought from their creation up to the end in all the major battles of the campaign. Adopting a commando approach, they raided some of the British first line positions at the very start of the Battle of Alexandria. Unfortunately, the main body of the unit was to surrender to the British

# THE FRENCH ARMY OF THE ORIENT 1798–1801

Andréossy, an artilleryman, was the grandson of a famous civil engineer and was naturally gifted in mathematics. This background made him close to Bonaparte who shared similar tastes.

given the hopelessness of the situation in Egypt. Bonaparte was not to forget this and Cavalier and his men, once back in France, were transferred to the Gendarmerie which effectively was mainly a local police force.

The Syrians

Under this rather generic term are grouped several units which in the end all merged into one and were listed as 'Syrians' in the last French orders of battle.

The very first one can hardly be called a military unit but reminds one more of a brutal collaborationist police force at the service of occupiers. At the start of the occupation of Cairo, after the Battle of the Pyramids, Bonaparte decided to use the services of a former Mameluke of Greek origin: Bartholomeo Serra, otherwise known in French sources as 'Barthelemy the Greek'. Flamboyant, fierce, and of a towering height, the man soon became the terror of the Cairo streets along with his band of some eighty former Mamelukes. He was also flanked by his spouse, by all accounts as striking and brutal as he was. Barthelemy's only task was police duty. He and his men were quite active following the first Cairo insurrection. They also rode out into Syria ensuring the safety of the army columns.

In Syria, a number of natives decided, willingly or not, to join the French troops. Some came from the garrison at El Arish, others after Jaffa. In any case, these troops followed the French back into Egypt where they were organised into two janissary companies. Kléber then decided to transform one of these into a 'company of mounted Syrian janissaries' under the command of Sheikh Yakub Habaily (23 September 1799). Once commander-in-chief, and satisfied with the performance of that unit, Menou created a second company under the command of Sheikh Yussef (7 July 1800). Each company was organised as follows: 3 native officers, 2 NCOs, 95 men and one French NCO.

Finally Menou decided to bring Barthelemy's force and those two companies into one unit on 26 October 1800 and named it 'Regiment of the Mamelukes of the Republic'. Barthelemy, promoted to the rank of chef de brigade, was at its head

Barthelemy and his wife had largely benefited materially from their actions. An as-yet-unpublished manuscript in the Orleans library indicates that Barthelemy's wife had come to ask Kléber for more rights to levy taxes on some lands. Kléber had conceded, provided she shared with him a very intimate moment. The author who had been witness to the scene from outside Kléber's room had then heard the lady screaming that the way Kléber was going about this specific action was 'un-natural'. This sheds some interesting lights on other aspects of Kléber's tastes!

# DOING MUCH WITH LITTLE: ORGANISATION AND TACTICS

The Battle of Aboukir by Duplessis-Bertaux. This drawing was published not too long after the event. Like Lejeune's painting, it is fairly accurate in terms of landscape, but shows the action at closer range, especially that of the artillery.

These Mamelukes of the Republic were to fight as part of Roize's cavalry at Alexandria. All the survivors sailed back for France and were temporarily set up in Marseille, until Bonaparte ordered one of his ADCs, Rapp, a veteran of Egypt, to organise them into a squadron which was to be integrated into the Consular Guard and therafter become the famous Mamelukes of the Guard. Barthelemy unfortunately had not lived to see this as he had died during the voyage to France.

The Coptic Legion (*La Légion Cophte*)

Copts are the original native Christian community of Egypt. They have constantly refused conversion to Islam. This had given them a unique position within society, being very active in anything dealing with finance and administration. From the start of the occupation of Egypt, the French were to rely on this part of the population for tax levying and other administrative duties. Obviously this did not make them popular and they were a prime target, especially during the second Cairo insurrection.

In September 1799, Kléber proposed to the leader of the community, Maallen Yakub, to form a Coptic Legion. Totalling some 800 men organised two battalions of five companies each, including one of grenadiers, it was placed under the command of a Copt, Gabriel Sidariu. Both the Greek and Coptic Legions were brought under the command of Chef de Brigade Coliquet who provided technical assistance.

The Copts tended to fare better than most of the other local units. During the 1801 campaign, they were however left in Cairo, although many Copts actually fought at Alexandria but in the ranks of the 21st Light Demi-brigade.

Like all the other native troops who had sided with the French they sailed back to France and, alongside their Greek comrades, they formed the new Chasseurs d'Orient.

Janissaries

All throughout their stay in Egypt, the French organised a number of local police forces usually called Janissaries. On 25 July 1798, Bonaparte ordered the creation of five Janissary companies to police Cairo and followed up on 17 July by ordering the raising of one company per province. These companies were of variable strength (for example, 25 in Suez, 50 in Belbeis). They had no specific uniform apart from wearing the tricolour cockade and were given a tricolour flag with an inscription in Arabic on one side, French on the other. There was no specific text for these, other than that they had to state 'something against the Mamelukes'!

Numerous other local forces came to French help during the Syrian campaign. Projects were then made by Bonaparte and his staff to raise forces amongst the Druze and Christian Maronite populations of modern-day Lebanon. All this remained theoretical following the failure in front of Acre.

National Guard

After the first Cairo insurrection, Bonaparte ordered the raising of ten companies of National Guards within the civilian European population. This seems never to have been realised. Once again, after the second insurrection, Kléber tried to raise a National Guard and a letter written in April 1800 by a certain Henri Wolmar asks for this to be done but it does not seem to have taken place. Finally Menou did likewise at the time of the Anglo-Ottoman invasion and especially during the siege of Alexandria. There is no proof that any of these units existed otherwise than on paper.

## Conclusion

French military organisation in Egypt was similar to other French military practices of the time when occupying a country. Much was made of trying to raise local contingents to help support the French war effort and as part of the Revolutionary fervour that was expected to grow.

However, unlike in Holland, Italy, or Germany, all of which were neighbours to France, the distance and cultural difference made such efforts difficult if not impossible. Furthermore, keeping the army at an adequate fighting level proved near impossible over time. The units which the British faced at the beginning of 1801 were those of 1798 only in name. Most of the best elements were gone. Makeshift replacements had been provided. Bonaparte had pushed his army to the edge. Once gone, his priorities shifted and he did not do much to ensure its survival. Kléber's remarkable actions built it back to an efficient fighting force which led to the victory at Heliopolis. Unfortunately, Menou had no comparable military gifts, even just for organisation. In effect, the army withered away as its morale dived.

# 4

# Lining up the Troops: Orders of Battle of the Army of the Orient 1798-1802

**The Army of the Orient, on Board the Fleet 6 June 1798**
This is compiled from a return drafted by the general paymaster (treasurer) of the army Estève while on board the Orient. This seems to be the most accurate document detailing the composition and strength of the Army of the Orient as it set out in the spring of 1798.

General staff:
    1 General-in-Chief
    11 Généraux de Division
    20 Généraux de Brigade
    13 General-Adjutants
    2 ADCs, Chefs de Brigade
    16 Chefs de battalion
    68 ADCs or 2nd ADCs, Captains
    12 Lieutenants
    Total General Staff: 143

Artillery staff
    3 Chefs de Brigade
    3 Chefs de Battalion
    8 First Captains, 8 Second Captains
    6 First Lieutenants, 10 Second Lieutenants
    2 First Guards, 2 Second (regular) Guards
    4 First Conductors, 21 Second (regular) Conductors
    Total artillery staff: 67

NB: artillery guards were in charge of securing the artillery when camped; conductors are artillery train conductors.

Engineer Staff
- 3 Chefs de Brigade
- 8 Chefs de Battalion
- 3 First Captains, 11 Second Captains
- 3 First Lieutenants, 2 Second Lieutenants
- 1 Third lieutenant (sub-lieutenant)
- 4 First aides, 3 Second aides (adjoints)
- 14 Secretaries or Writer-Draughtsmen
- 1 Manager, 2 Store-keepers
- 3 Conductors, 8 Horse servants
- Total engineer staff: 66

Commissariat of War
- 1 Commissary-in-Chief (commissaire ordonnateur en chef)
- 8 War Commissaries First Class
- 17 War Commissaries Second Class
- Total commissariat of war: 26

Health Services
- 3 Health Officers-in-Chief
- 30 Health Officers First Class
- 25 Health Officers Second Class
- 110 Health Officers Third Class
- Total health services: 168

Army Treasury
- 35 General Paymasters
- 6 Controllers
- Total army treasury: 41

Army Administration
- 105 in the first supplies section
- 100 in the second supplies section
- 142 in hospitals
- 35 in clothing
- 20 in artillery train
- 21 in transports train
- 22 in postal services
- Total army administration: 445

Scientists & Artists
- 21 Mathematicians
- 3 Astronomers
- 15 Natural Scientists & Mining Engineers
- 17 Civil Engineers
- 15 Geographers
- 4 Architects
- 3 Construction Engineering Students

## LINING UP THE TROOPS: ORDERS OF BATTLE OF THE ARMY OF THE ORIENT 1798-1802

8 Draughtsmen
1 Sculptor
10 Mechanical 'Artists'
3 Gunpowder & Explosives Specialists
10 Writers & Secretaries
15 Consuls & Interpreters
9 Health Officers, 9 Nurses
22 Printing Specialists
2 musicians
Total scientists & artists: 167

Guides
   300 on foot, 180 mounted = 480

Light Infantry
   2nd Light Demi-Brigade = 1,368
   4th Light Demi-Brigade = 1,016
   21st Light Demi-Brigade = 2,000
   22nd Light Demi-Brigade = 1,019
   Total light infantry = 5,403

Line Infantry
   9th Line Demi-Brigade = 1,509
   13th Line Demi-Brigade = 2,430
   18th Line Demi-Brigade = 1,550
   19th Line Demi-Brigade = 1,500
   25th Line Demi-Brigade = 1,530
   32nd Line Demi-Brigade = 1,850
   61st Line Demi-Brigade = 1,800
   69th Line Demi-Brigade = 1,500
   75th Line Demi-Brigade = 1,700
   85th Line Demi-Brigade = 1,720
   88th Line Demi-Brigade = 1,500
   6th Line Demi-Brigade, 1 battalion = 520
   80th demi-brigade, 1 battalion &
      3 grenadier companies = 560
   Total line infantry = 19,669

Mounted Troops
   7th bis Hussars = 600
   22nd Chasseurs = 250
   3rd Dragoons = 360
   14th Dragoons = 600
   15th Dragoons = 200
   18th Dragoons = 300
   20th Dragoons = 500
   Total mounted troops = 2,810

Berthier. This splendid engraving by Ruotte shows Berthier in the full regalia of his general's uniform. Berthier was throughout his career a superb chief-of-staff and if we can today go through fairly detailed orders of battle, it is very much thanks to his own work as an organiser.

Artillery & engineers
| | | |
|---|---|---|
| Sappers | = | 776 |
| Miners | = | 192 |
| Balloon corps | = | 25 |
| Engineering workers | = | 164 |
| Horse artillery | = | 485 |
| Foot artillery | = | 888 |
| Demi-brigade gunners | = | 388 |
| Artillery workers | = | 237 |
| Total artillery & engineers | = | 3,245 |

This also totals up to 32,730 men, not including unit officers. The grand total is 35,000, but to this one needs to add one battalion of the 7th Light Demi-Brigade which boarded at the last minute and the troops of the 41st Line Demi-Brigade which were doing ship defence duty.

7th Light Demi-Brigade = 1,174
41st Line Demi-Brigade = 371

The grand 'military' total therefore comes up to 36,545: adding civilian train personnel the estimate comes to 38,000 to which one can add servants, women etc. Overall, the entire fleet transported probably 40,000 individuals.

In terms of horses, going through the various boarding returns, the number carried did not exceed 1230. Assuming 250 were allocate to the general staff and 250 to the artillery, this left around 700 horses for the cavalry! Only a quarter of the cavalry could be mounted. The assumption was that an ample supply of horses would be readily found in Egypt.

Artillery equipment
A total of 171 pieces of artillery boarded from Europe. As we know the regular French artillery system was the one introduced just recently by Gribeauval.

It was divided in field, siege, and coastal pieces (the last category not used here):

Field: 4, 8 and 12 pounder guns, 6-inch howitzer
Siege: 4 (long), 8, 12, 16 & 24 pounder guns, 8-inch howitzer.
Mortars came as 8, 10, and 12-inch versions and came from various systems introduced since 1765.

Interestingly, the returns show a much greater variety of equipment. In fact the French had captured a significant amount of ordinance from the Austrians, Piedmontese-Sardinians and other minor Italian states. These had been pressed into service, especially the light 3- and 5-pounders (the latter actually 6-pounders according to Austrian or Piedmontese measurements) of which the equivalents were to some degree lacking in the French army.

| | | |
|---|---|---|
| *Siege Artillery* | = | 35 |
| 24-pounder | = | 28 |

# LINING UP THE TROOPS: ORDERS OF BATTLE OF THE ARMY OF THE ORIENT 1798-1802

| | | |
|---|---|---|
| 20-pounder | = | 2 |
| 16-pounder | = | 5 |
| *Field Artillery* | = | 72 |
| 12-pounder | = | 17 |
| 11-pounder | = | 2 |
| 8-pounder | = | 35 |
| 5-pounder | = | 6 |
| 3-pounder | = | 12 |
| *Field Howitzers* | = | 24 |
| 8-inch | = | 4 |
| 6-inch | = | 20 |
| *Siege Mortars* | = | 40 |
| 12-inch | = | 15 |
| 10-inch | = | 4 |
| 8-inch | = | 18 |
| 5 ¼-inch | = | 3 |

In support of all this, the following caissons were also transported:

Caissons

| | | |
|---|---|---|
| 12-pounder caisson | = | 69 |
| 11-pounder caisson | = | 6 |
| 8-pounder caisson | = | 74 |
| 3-pounder caisson | = | 12 |
| Howitzer caisson | = | 113 |
| Infantry caisson | = | 111 |
| Artillery park caisson | = | 53 |

Wurst Carts

| | | |
|---|---|---|
| 8-pounder cart | = | 27 |
| Howitzer cart | = | 17 |
| Ammunition Cart | = | 183 |
| Gun cart | = | 65 |
| Forge to heat up cannonballs | = | 5 |
| Field forge | = | 20 |
| Mountain forge | = | 2 |

Guide (foot) of the Army of the Orient. The guides provided protection and general service to the headquarters. We do not have actual contemporary iconography from Egypt, so this is a reconstruction by Pierre Benigni done for the Bucquoy cards series.

A total of 757 various wagons were therefore also put on board, but this was not all, one can find in the returns:

9 field-repair cart (chèvre)
65 stretchers
179 ladders
599,150 sand bags
6,775 square shovels
3,869 round shovels
7,339 picks

576 rock picks
3,005 sickles
2,786 axes
6,650 muskets
550 bayonets

To carry the army a fleet of some 280 ships had been assembled.

Thirteen ships of the line provided the bulk of the fighting power:

The *Orient*, a massive very recent three-decker, launched in 1792 it had been named *Dauphin-Royal* and then renamed *Sans-Culotte*. In 1795, it had become the *Orient*, an interesting coincidence given its unforeseen future. With 120 guns and 1,130 crewmen it struck everyone who mounted on board in May 1798 as a 'real city' with sailors and soldiers running in all directions. The day of the Battle of Aboukir (The Nile) it was being repainted and it seems that the paint which was on board accelerated the fire which had started and prevented it being extinguished, leading to its explosion. Its remains were located in 1984 in Aboukir Bay, some 7 kilometres from the shoreline.

The *Guillaume-Tell*, *Franklin*, and *Tonnant* had 80 guns and a crew of 866 men. The *Tonnant* was commanded by Captain Dupetit-Thouars who died bleeding to death almost limbless at Aboukir urging his men not to surrender the ship.

*Spartiate*, *Aquilon*, *Peuple-Souverain*, *Généreux*, *Guerrier*, *Timoléon*, *Heureux*, and *Mercure* were all 74-gun ships with a crew each of 706 men. The *Conquérant* also had 74 guns, but of a lesser calibre given its old age, and only 560 men.

6 frigates provided lesser firing power:

*Justice*, *Diane*, and *Junon*, 40 guns, 18-pounder main battery, 340 men each

*Artémise*, 40 guns, 12-pounder main battery, 282 men

*Alceste* and *Sérieuse*, 36 guns, 12-pounder main battery, 270 men each

One light vessel was also armed, the *Badine* with 30 guns and an 8-pounder main battery. The other ships were either lightly armed or not at all if they were civilian trade vessels.

Of all the fighting fleet only the *Guillaume-Tell* and *Généreux* survived the Battle of Aboukir Bay along with the frigates *Justice* and *Diane*. *Orient*, *Timoléon*, *Sérieuse* and *Artémise* were sunk. *Guerrier*, *Heureux*, and *Mercure* were captured but too badly damaged, and ultimately had to be destroyed by the British.

*Conquérant* became HMS *Conquerant*
*Spartiate* became HMS *Spartiate*
*Aquilon* became HMS *Aboukir*
*Peuple-Souverain* became HMS *Guerrier*
*Franklin* became HMS *Canopus*
*Tonnant* Became HMS *Tonnant*

Of the French lighter vessels and gunboats, their participation in the main battle was limited and they provided the bulk of the remaining French fleet in Egypt.

## Vaubois' occupation force in Malta and Maltese Troops

On 14 June 1798, Bonaparte issued the order which details which forces were to remain in Malta under the command of General Vaubois. This became known as the 'Division Vaubois'.

| | | |
|---|---|---|
| 7th Light Demi-Brigade | = | 900 |
| 6th Line Demi-Brigade | = | 518 |
| 41st Line Demi-Brigade | = | 285 |
| 80th Line Demi-Brigade | = | 650 |
| 19th Line Demi-Brigade | = | 700 |
| Total | = | 3,053 men |

Of the 19th Line Demi-Brigade, only the 2nd and 3rd battalions were left in Malta, the 1st battalion and the 3 grenadier companies remained with the main force. The 1st battalion was to replace the 41st line demi-brigade troops on board the ships. The 3 grenadier companies were to be ultimately assigned on 3 July 1798 to reinforce the general staff escort in addition to the Guides. They were put under the direct command of Bessières.

38 French Knights of Malta agreed to follow the expedition into Egypt and they were used in various duties.

Maltese troops were incited to join the French service. 119 grenadiers from the Guard of the Grand-Master of the Order decided to follow. As many were married and had children, those families were accepted on board. A total of 358 men from the Regiment of Malta also followed. So, in total, 477 Maltese troops followed forming what was to become the Maltese Legion. Those two units were the best which Malta had to offer, although many officers and NCOs were 50 years or more of age. As stated elsewhere, the Maltese Legion was far from being a very effective fighting corps and quite a few Maltese deserted as we can tell from the daily army orders.

## Organisation of the Army at the landing, 23-28 June 1798

A few days before the landing, Bonaparte organised his army. This organisation is important as it laid much of the foundation for the weeks and months that were to follow.

He appointed some his key generals to head up each division. Given the number of généraux de brigade, the light demi-brigades were under the command of some on top of their regular chef de brigade. After the initial order on the 23rd, a few changes were made and so the reader will find what seems to have been the final state of organisation.

Division Kléber
    2nd Light DB = General Verdier
    25th & 75th Line DBs = General Lannes
    General Damas, chief of staff

Engineers: Chef de Battalion Cazals, Captain Ferrus, 1 officer and 46 sappers from the 4th company of the Milan battalion

Division Desaix
   21st Light DB = General Belliard
   61st & 88th Line DBs = General Friant
   Adjutant-General Donzelot, chief of staff
   Engineers: Captain Garbé, Lieutenant Deponthon, 1 officer and 50 sappers from the 8th company of the Milan battalion.

Division Bon
   4th Light DB = General Marmont
   18th & 32nd Line DBs = General Rampon
   Adjutant-General Valentin, chief of staff
   Engineers: Captain Bertrand, Lieutenant Crespin, 1 officer and 50 sappers from the 7th company of the Milan battalion.

Division Menou
   22nd Light DB = General Veaux
   13th & 69th Line DBs = General Vial
   Adjutant-General Rambaud, chief of staff
   Engineers: Captains Rivierieux & Micheux, 3 officers and 48 sappers from the 5th company of the 6th battalion.

Division Reynier
   9th & 85th Line DBs = General Fugière
   Adjutant-General Jullien, chief of staff
   Engineers: Captain Geoffroy, Lieutenant Burel, 1 officer and 50 sappers from the 7th company of the Milan battalion.

Mounted Troops
   Général de Division Dumas commands all the cavalry of the army
   Adjutant-General Devaux and Adjutant-General Alméras, joint chiefs of staff
   (Note that the fact there were two men posted to seemingly the same role may seem odd, but such is the case. In practice they divided up their own role to support the division. Overall, there was an 'over-supply' of senior officers, to account for possible future losses)
   7th *bis* Hussars and 3rd Dragoons = General Leclerc
   22nd Chasseurs and 20th Dragoons = General Mireur
   14th and 15th Dragoons = General Murat
   18th Dragoons = General Davout

General Dugua is charged with army inspection
General Dommartin commands the artillery
General Songis commands the artillery park
General Caffarelli commands the engineers
General Andreossy commands the pontoon section

# LINING UP THE TROOPS: ORDERS OF BATTLE OF THE ARMY OF THE ORIENT 1798-1802

150 sappers from the 5th company of the 6th battalion of engineers are attached to the pontoon section under the command of Captain Dodet, with Ferco and Collet as aides.

Generals Dumuy & Zayonchek are attached to the general headquarters

Sucy is the commissary in chief of the army

## The Attack on Alexandria, 2 July 1798

Given the rough landing, only the divisions of Kléber, Menou, and Bon were available to attack, having approximately 5000 men between them. Reynier, whose division had started landing, was ordered to continue and defend the landing spot.

The 69th Line Demi-Brigade was to provide the bulk of the Alexandria garrison. As both Kléber and Menou had been wounded in the assault, they were left behind while the main force proceeded on to Cairo.

Kléber was to command Alexandria and Aboukir. The command of his division was given to General Dugua. As for Menou, he was sent to occupy and command Rosetta with Dugua's division. In his stead, Vial is given Menou's division to command.

All the five divisions: Bon, Desaix, Reynier, Dugua, and Vial participated in both the battles of Chebreiss and the Pyramids. Each was set up for as a large square, in fact a rectangle to fight the charging Mameluke cavalry.

Guide (mounted) of the Army of the Orient. Gradually the mounted guides adopted local equipment and dress. In this reconstruction by Begnini, the guide has a locally-sourced saddle and harness as well as what is called an 'Arab coat' in contemporary archival sources.

## Situation of the Army of the Orient as of 18 August 1798

This is the first true detailed return of the entire Army of the Orient that the French archives still have. It gives a large amount of detail and covers all the units under the command of Bonaparte. This includes not only Egypt and Malta, but also Corsica and Corfu. Only the troops present in Egypt are given here

Oddly enough, as all too often with the documents found in the archives, there are still some omissions: the staff, the administration, the guides, and the grenadiers of the 19th are not included; nor is the artillery reserve. Still, it totals up (civilians not included) to about 33,000 men. If one accounts for the troops in Malta, the actual losses of the army at mid-August 1798 are of 'only' 800 men, this being somewhat compensated by the Maltese and sailors who had survived Aboukir.

Each main body (division or otherwise) is indicated with the detail of its units with figures given in the form total men available/men ready for service, as well as figures for horses

1st Division – General Dugua (formerly Kléber's)
Généraux de Brigade: Damas, Verdier, Destaing
War Commissary: Raymondon

| | | |
|---|---|---|
| 25th Line DB (3 battalions) | = | 1,588/1,296, 6 horses (officers') |
| 75th Line DB (3 battalions) | = | 2,039/1,692, 4 horses (officers') |
| 2nd Light DB (3 battalions) | = | 1,705/1,194, 11 horses (officers') |
| Artillery | = | 68/51 |
| Sappers | = | 48/41 |
| Total | = | 5448/4274, 21 horses (officers') |

The difference of 1,174 men between those available for service and those not, can be explained by over 500 being in hospitals and another close to 500 being on service on board some of the Nile flotilla.

2nd Division – General Bon
Généraux de Brigade: Rampon, Marmont
Adjutant-Generals: Sornet, Valentin
War Commissary: Bouquin

| | | |
|---|---|---|
| 18th Line DB (3 battalions) | = | 1,408/1,271, 8 horses (officers') |
| 32nd Line DB (3 battalions) | = | 1,593/1,450, 18 horses (officers') |
| 4th Light DB (3 battalions) | = | 1,147/973, 23 horses (officers') |
| 6th Coy, 4th Artillery Regt. | = | 66/59 |
| Detachment 8th Light Artillery | = | 32/27 |
| Sappers, 5th battalion | = | 52/44 |
| Total | = | 4298/3824, 49 horses (officers') |

The difference of 474 men between those available for service and those not is almost fully explained by the number of men in hospitals: 354

3rd Division – General Reynier
Général de Brigade: Lagrange
Adjutant-Generals: Beauvais, Devaux
War Commissary: Duprat; aide, Segnoret

| | | |
|---|---|---|
| 9th Line DB (3 battalions) | = | 1,609/1,430 |
| 85th Line DB (3 battalions) | = | 2,627/1,488 |
| Detachment 4th Artillery | = | 22/22 |
| Detachment 4th Light Artillery | = | 42/40 |
| Sappers, 4 Coys, 5th battalion | = | 387/249 |
| Total | = | 4687/3229 |

A total of 1458 men are not available for service, 601 are in hospital, 262 are on leave, and 187 are on service on board the Nile flotilla.

4th Division – General Desaix
Généraux de Brigade: Friant, Belliard
Adjutant-General: Donzelot
War Commissaries: Sartelot, Daure

| | | |
|---|---|---|
| 61st Line DB (3 battalions) | = | 1,930/1,690 |
| 88th Line DB (3 battalions) | = | 1,284/1,164 |

21st Light DB (3 battalions) = 1,923/1,629
11th Coy, 1st Artillery Regt = 65/35
5th Coy, 1st Light Artillery = 67/45, 38 horses (troopers')
Sappers = 49/49
Total = 5318/4612, 38 horses (troopers')

Out of 706 men not on service, 188 are in hospitals, 120 detached, and 84 on board the Nile flotilla.

5th Division – General Lannes (was Menou's and then Vial's)
Général de Brigade: Veaux
Adjutant-General: Rambaud
War Commissary: Chauvot

13th Line DB (3 battalions) = 2,287/1,580, 10 horses (officers')
22nd Light DB (3 battalions) = 1,301/1,123, 14 horses (officers')
3rd Coy, 4th Light Artillery = 84/73, 30 horses (4 officers', 26 troopers')
5th Coy, 6th Battalion Sappers = 63/49
Total = 3735/2825, 54 horses

Out of 910 men not on service, 458 are in hospitals, 115 are on leave, and 200 on board the Nile flotilla.

Cavalry Division: General Dumas
Généraux de Brigade: Davout, Leclerc, Murat, Zayonchek
Adjutant-General: Alméras
War Commissary: Grobet

3rd Dragoons = 376/139, 162 horses (39 officers', 123 troopers')
14th Dragoons = 516/436, 120 horses (20 officers', 100 troopers')
15th Dragoons = 354/205, 121 horses (30 officers', 90 troopers')
18th Dragoons = 381/197, 19 horses (3 officers', 16 troopers')
20th Dragoons = 557/332, 74 horses (14 officers', 60 troopers')
22nd Chasseurs = 318/179, 150 horses (33 officers', 117 troopers')
7th *bis* Hussars = 413/191, 200 horses (51 officers', 149 troopers')
Total cavalry = 2,915/1,677, 846 horses.

Given the limited amount of horses to be had, much of the cavalry is detached for garrison service or similar, totalling 1077 men; 108 are in hospital.

Alexandria Garrison: General Kléber
Adjutant-General: Escale
War Commissary: Colasse

69th Line DB = 1,902/1,497
Artillery = 140/126

Total         = 2,042/1,623

Out of the 419 men not on service, 126 are on board the fleet, 213 in hospital

Overall the return shows a force of 28,443 men, with 22,064 available for service and 1,008 horses. Close to nine per cent of the force is in hospital with the 3rd and 5th division reaching a level of 12-13 per cent%. As stated, this return does not include some other available forces: guides, grenadiers of the 19th DB, and sailors. It does however paint an accurate picture of the challenges the French were facing at the beginning of their conquest: much of the cavalry was still dismounted, few men had died, but many were already in hospitals.

## Desaix' Division as it set out for Upper-Egypt – 26 August 1798

Desaix set out basically with part of his division so a little less than 3,000 men, two light guns and some sappers.

21st Light DB = 1,182
    1st battalion = 595
    2nd battalion = 587

61st Line DB = 987
    1st battalion = 488
    2nd battalion = 427
    3rd battalion grenadiers = 72

88th Line DB = 608
    1st battalion = 289
    2nd battalion = 319

Infantry total = 2777
Artillery: detachment 5th Coy, 1st Artillery = 32
Artillery train = 30
Engineers = 1 captain and 22 sappers

In total 2,862 men with two 5-pounder guns, three 5-pounder caissons, and 23 horses.

Friant joined the expedition, but not Belliard who had fallen ill with ophthalmia.

By 21 September 1798, another detachment of men from the 3rd battalion of the 21st Light DB was sent out to reinforce Desaix with a little over 300 men. Although there is no precise trace of it, another artillery piece was sent (a howitzer). On that date, Desaix' command was composed of 154 officers and 2,984 men, so 3,138 in total.

Donzelot, his adjutant-general, indicates the following in the return after the battle of Sediman:

# LINING UP THE TROOPS: ORDERS OF BATTLE OF THE ARMY OF THE ORIENT 1798-1802

21st Light DB (3 battalions)
    Present = 1368
    Dead = 33

61st Line DB (2 battalions + grenadiers from 3rd battalion)
    Present = 916
    Dead = 1

88th Line DB (2 battalions)
    Present = 594
    Dead = 1

Artillery = 61

Train
    Present = 35
    Dead = 1

Sappers = 12
Workers = 4

A total of 2,990 men and 22 horses, two 5-pounder guns and one howitzer.

The fatalities of Sediman amount to 36 with the bulk coming from the 21st Light DB which had to leave its wounded behind as it formed the square.

One will note there are some inconsistencies between the first return and the one made after Sediman. As Donzelot's post-action return does not distinguish those who had recently been sent to hospital or were detached from those who did not participate at the start of the expedition, this explains the differences.

## Davout's Reinforcement Force for Desaix – 6 December 1798

Early December, Bonaparte finally decided to send cavalry to Desaix so that the latter could go after Murad-Bey more efficiently. He committed to this force most of the troops he had been able to mount.

7th *bis* Hussars = chef de brigade, 1 chef d'escadron, & 200 troopers
22nd Chasseurs = chef de brigade, 1 chef d'escadron, & 220 troopers
15th Dragoons = chef de brigade, 1 chef d'escadron, & 160 troopers
18th Dragoons = 1 chef d'escadron & 100 troopers
20th Dragoons = chef de brigade, 1 chef d'escadron, & 160 troopers
24th Dragoons = 1 chef d'escadron & 100 troopers
3 light artillery pieces and their crews.

This column of about 1,000 men reached Desaix on 10 December 1798.

We have a detailed return of Desaix' division, dated 15 December 1798. By then Belliard who was now feeling well had joined:

Reynier, probably one of the best generals – if not the best– left after Kléber's death. Reynier was a proven division commander, but also well known for his bad temper. His falling-out with Menou did not help his career. He suffered yet another setback against British forces at Maida in 1806. After that he held several commands in 1809 and then in Spain 1810-1811 and finally Russia. He suffered setbacks at times, victories at others, but his career was never stellar. He died 'of exhaustion' in early 1814. His pamphlet-book *De l'Égypte après la bataille d'Héliopolis* remains one of the very best sources on the organisation of the army after Kléber.

# THE FRENCH ARMY OF THE ORIENT 1798–1801

Friant, who was to rise as one of Davout's well known division commanders and later command part of the Old Guard at Waterloo, was already a 'veteran' in Egypt at the ripe age of 40!

Commander: Général de Division Desaix
ADCs = Savary, Rapp, Clément

Généraux de Brigade:
Friant: ADCs, Binot, Petit
Belliard: ADCs, Parat, Majou
Davout: ADC, Saint-Léger

Adjutant-generals
Donzelot: aide, Donzelot
Rabasse: aide, Galoteau

Artillery Commander: Chef de Brigade Latourneau
Engineers: Captain Garbé

Artillery:
Five 8 pounder guns with five caissons
Two 5 pounder guns with two caissons
One 3 pounder gun and one caisson
One 6 pounder howitzer and one caisson
Two ammunition carts
One field forge

Each infantry battalion has one camel, the same for each cavalry regiment.
Infantry

61st Line DB
 (1st & 2nd battalions plus grenadiers from 3rd battalion)
 Officers = 39
 Men = 625

88th Line DB
 (1st and 2nd battalions)
 Officers = 66
 Men = 874

21st Light DB
 (All three battalions)
 Officers = 61
 Men = 1,427

Total infantry = 3,092
Officers = 166
Men = 2,926

Cavalry
 14th Dragoons = 8 officers, 100 troopers, 119 horses
 15th Dragoons = 21 officers, 155 troopers, 205 horses

18th Dragoons = 9 officers, 90 troopers, 101 horses
20th Dragoons = 20 officers, 162 troopers, 184 horses
7th *bis* Hussars = 19 officers, 191 troopers, 237 horses
22nd Chasseurs = 27 men, 199 troopers, 255 horses
Detachment from 3rd Dragoons = 2 officers and 44 troopers
Detachment from 7th *bis* Hussars = 3 officers and 47 troopers
(both these detachments had been actually sent dismounted to get horses)
Cavalry total = 1,097
Officers = 109
Troopers = 988

Artillery & Engineers = 119 men
5th Company, 3rd Artillery = 3 officers, 58 men
7th Company, 8th Light Artillery = 25 men
Sappers = 33

In total, Desaix's force was composed of 278 officers and 4,030 men – still a rather small force but now with enough cavalry to be able to exploit any victory by chasing up the Mamelukes.

Interestingly enough, multiple witnesses agree on Davout's obvious ambition. He did not seem to hide that all he wanted was to quickly shine on the battlefield and get promoted to Général de Division. This is probably one of the reasons he undertook several unjustified risks throughout the campaign. When one knows how disciplined and organised Davout was to become later, these comments paint a rather unusual image of this great military leader still in his youth.

At Redecieh on 11 February 1799, Davout fought with the 15th Dragoons and 22nd Chasseurs against the Mamelukes. The 15th had 24 killed (including 4 officers) and 31 wounded, the 22nd 13 killed (including 2 officers) and 13 wounded. Given the few cavalry available in Egypt, although a tactical victory this can be equalled to a strategic setback. The 15th had lost almost 20 per cent of its officers killed and 31 per cent of its overall force killed or wounded, the 22nd, 12 per cent! Lasalle, chef de brigade of the 22nd and future famous leader of light cavalry during the Empire was to complain bitterly in a letter to Dugua: 'This general had my temper so heated that it almost reached the point a man of honour has to come to, but he is yet of such a moderate temper to really have had such a conduct'. Lasalle blamed it all finally on Davout's inexperience and his sheer ambition, yet acknowledged that he was not a hot-head. Happily for both, Lasalle did not get to the point of having a duel with his commanding officer!

## Bonaparte's Expedition to Suez

In December of 1798, Bonaparte decided to explore Suez and what remained of the ancient canal there. Suez had been ignored by the French, was not yet occupied, and could prove potentially an excellent trade harbour. Therefore, Bonaparte's trip to Suez became an interesting adventure combining scientific, economic, and military goals.

Bonaparte first dispatched a force on to Suez, where it arrived on 11 December:

32nd Line DB, 2nd battalion = 24 officers, 487 men
85th Line DB gunners = 2 officers, 36 men
Milan Battalion Sappers = 15 men
7th *bis* hussars = 12 troopers, 12 horses
Omar's Turkish company = 1 officer, 114 troopers
Horses for the staff = 19 horses
Artillery Train = 3 officers, 24 men,
Engineers: 1 officer, 1 civilian engineer, 1 aide
Transport Train: 5 employees, 50 Turks, 117 camels
Ambulance: 9 men
Artillery: Two 3-pounder guns

This small force of approximately 700 men ensured that Suez was occupied and secured. As one will note, it made good use of some of the first native troops under French service, in the shape of 'Omar's Turkish company'.

It was only after Suez and Katieh had been occupied that Bonaparte himself set out. He took with him his key subordinates:

Berthier, chief of staff
Dommartin, artillery commander
Caffarelli, engineer commander
Ganteaume, fleet commander
Daure, chief war commissary

He had with him a personal escort of 100 mounted guides and 200 guides on foot plus an artillery piece.

Bonaparte was back in Cairo on 7 January and, as Berthier wrote to Menou, it was a scouting expedition, exploring the ancient canal and chasing whoever was unfriendly, capturing 180 Arabs along with some of their camels, and burning their camp. One of the most direct consequences of this expedition was that Bonaparte, seeing a Sheik on a dromedary, noticed that it seemed an efficient means of transport. He asked his ADCs, Leturq and Beauharnais, to try mounting such animals. Seeing how fast they could go, this decided him to organise the Dromedary Regiment in early January, in time for the Syrian expedition.

## The Syrian Campaign

With the Syrian campaign, the Army of the Orient went back on the offensive. Apart from Desaix' venture into Upper Egypt and occasional guerrilla activity against Mamelukes and Arabs, the bulk of the troops has not fought since the Pyramids in the summer. The campaign was to prove much harder than anyone had anticipated. This can also be seen through the absence of regular precise troop returns. When digging into the archives, one is faced with a quasi-absence of detailed documents until after Menou assumed command. It is possible that some reports might be tucked away in correspondence boxes. However given some of the extremely thorough work done by French military historians before the First World War, it is quite likely that these returns, if there were any, have not survived or else they would have been unearthed during that process.

Still, one can piece together a fairly good image of the force that marched into Syria and what happened to it. A one page document, written in Cairo after the campaign, summarises the situation quite well. 9 February 1799 is a week after the date on which the campaign started; 15 May is when the army ended the siege of Acre and started its retreat.

| Units | 9 February 1799 | 15 May 1799 | Difference | % Loss |
|---|---|---|---|---|
| Division Kléber | 2,349 | 1,800 | -449 | 19.1% |
| Division Bon | 2,499 | 1,509 | -740 | 29.6% |
| Division Lannes | 2,924 | 1,716 | -908 | 31,1% |
| Division Reynier | 2,160 | 1,522 | -638 | 29.5% |
| Cavalry | 800 | 700 | -100 | 12.5% |
| Artillery | 1,385 | 1,080 | -305 | 22.0% |
| Engineers | 340 | 272 | -68 | 20.0% |
| Guides | 400 | 333 | -67 | 16.8% |
| Dromedaries | 88 | 88 | 0 | 0.0% |
| 22nd Light DB | | 300 | 300 | |
| 25th Line DB, 1st Bat. | | 100 | 100 | |
| 4th Light DB, Bat. sent to Cairo | | 250 | 250 | |
| Total | 12,945 | 9,670 | -3,275 | 25.3% |

To this one must add

Headquarters & staff = 65
French servants = 245
Administration & supplies = 115

Marching into Syria, the army amounted to 13,370 men, probably not counting any native servants (as the document clearly spells out the servants as 'French'). We have no indication of the losses for the last three categories listed, but what we can see is that the army lost a quarter of its force (note that the individual infantry units detached as of 15 May have been re-incorporated in their respective divisions to compute the individual losses). Losses were fairly heavy for infantry (as one would expect) but also for artillery and engineers. This is of course not too surprising as much of the campaign amounted to siege warfare.

The document also gives a breakdown of the 3,275 losses. There are about 2,000 which are actually wounded or sick (15 per cent of the force), 500 died of fever (4 per cent), leaving 775, or 6 per cent of the total force, having died in combat. This reflects with force the hardships of the Syrian campaign.

As for the exact breakdown of the force by division:

# THE FRENCH ARMY OF THE ORIENT 1798–1801

Dromedary. Coloured print by Eugene Lami. Published in 1821 (the year of Napoleon's death), the series of prints devoted to the French army by Horace Vernet and Eugene Lami (with a few done by Carle Vernet, Horace's father) is one of the very first formal works of its kind in France. It is also the very first publication which has actually a chapter devoted to the Army of the Orient and its uniforms. The dromedary here is probably fairly fanciful as regards its headdress (a regular Napoleonic shako) but is otherwise probably accurate.

Division Kléber
Généraux de Brigade Verdier & Junot
2nd Light DB
25th Line DB, 2 battalions
75th Line DB, 2 battalions

Division Reynier
Général de Brigade Lagrange
9th Line DB
85th Line DB

Division Bon
Généraux de Brigade Rampon & Vial
4th Light DB, 1st battalion
18th Line DB, 1st & 2nd battalions
32nd Line DB, 1st & 2nd battalions

Division Lannes
Généraux de Brigade Veaux & Robin
22nd Light DB, 1st battalion
13th Line DB, 1st and 2nd battalions
69th Line DB, 1st & 2nd battalions

Murat's Cavalry
7th *bis* Hussars: 1 squadron
22nd Chasseurs: 1 squadron
3rd Dragoons
14th Dragoons
18th Dragoons
20th Dragoons: 1 squadron
For a total of around 800 men.

We do not have the detail of the artillery pieces which left with the army by land, but we do have a status of how many pieces were in front of Acre on 5 May 1799, just prior to the army leaving Acre.

Siege Guns
    32-pounder: 1
    24-pounders: 3
    18-pounders mounted on navy carriages: 6

Field guns
    12-pounders: 5
    8-pounders: 6
    4-pounders: 9 (of which 4 were out of service)

Howitzers
    6-pounders: 3

Turkish howitzers: 5
So, a total of 38 guns.

In addition, in October of 1799 a list of the guns lots in Syria was drafted in Cairo

Siege guns:
   24 pounders: 5, of which 2 were of cast iron
   18 pounder: 6
   16 pounder: 2
   9 pounder howitzer, cast iron: 1

The two cast-iron 24-pounders and the two 16-pounders were lost to the British in the harbour of Haifa.

Field guns:
   12 pounders: 4
   8 pounders: 5
   3 pounders: 3
   6 pounder howitzers: 5

So the army lost a total of 31 guns in Syria.

One cannot tell if the 38 guns in front of Acre included some of the lost ordinance which is reported in October 1799. One has to bear in mind that there was some confusion between the various 3 and 4-pounder calibres. In any case, it is quite probable the army carried into Syria about 60 artillery pieces and lost therefore close to 50 per cent, a rather appalling statistic. Obviously Conte's men were put to good use after the campaign to ensure the Army of Orient artillery was back in shape.

## The Battle of Aboukir

Aboukir was the last battle fought by Bonaparte in Egypt, before we look in detail into the order of battle, there is a document in the French war archives which gives an overview of the evolution of the Army of Orient strength. It is dated 15 July 1799. That date is not innocent as on 27 June, so about two weeks before, the full organisation of the demi-brigades was changed, precisely because of the losses incurred.

| Unit | Departure from France (6 May 1798) | Arrival in Egypt (2 July 1798) | Start of Syrian campaign (2 February 1799) | 15 July 1799 |
|---|---|---|---|---|
| 9th Line DB | 1,607 | 1,573 | 1,496 | 1,171 |
| 13th Line DB | 2,027 | 2,008 | 1,826 | 1,335 |
| 18th Line DB |  |  |  | 956 |
| 19th Line DB |  |  |  | 332 |
| 25th Line DB | 1,221 | 1,219 | 1,182 | 1,085 |
| 32nd Line DB |  | 1,903 |  | 1,442 |
| 61st Line DB | 1,619 | 1,596 |  | 1,478 |

# THE FRENCH ARMY OF THE ORIENT 1798–1801

| Unit | Departure from France (6 May 1798) | Arrival in Egypt (2 July 1798) | Start of Syrian campaign (2 February 1799) | 15 July 1799 |
|---|---|---|---|---|
| 69th Line DB | 1,549 | 1,539 | 1,817* | 1,571 |
| 75th Line DB | 1,972 | 1,938 | 1,814 | 1,568 |
| 85th Line DB | 1,883 | 1,881 | 1,720 | 1,430 |
| 88th Line DB | 1,330 | 1,307 | 1,230 | 1,230 |
| 2nd Light DB | 1,472 | 1,379 | 1,269 | 13,40** |
| 4th Light DB | 1,134 | 1,132 | 1,192* | 893 |
| 21st Light DB |  | 1,123 | 2,152* | 1,426 |
| 22nd Light DB | 1,230 | 1,228 | 1,278* | 1,127 |
| 3rd Dragoons | 390 | 390 | 364 | 329 |
| 14th Dragoons | 470 | 454 | 430 | 405 |
| 15th Dragoons | 257 |  | 241 | 208 |
| 18th Dragoons | 294 | 294 | 231 | 194 |
| 20th Dragoons | 415 | 411 | 391 | 374 |
| 22nd Chasseurs | 404 | 385 | 411* | 369 |
| 7th bis Hussars |  |  |  | 592 |
| Artillery | 3,447 | 3,143 | 3,410* | 3,117 |
| Engineers | 1,177 | 1,154 | 1,006 | 977 |
| Balloon Corps | 31 | 31 | 31 | 30 |

\* Sailors added to the unit

\*\* 184 grenadiers from the 19th Line DB transferred to the 2nd Light DB

As one can see, some of the starting figures do not necessarily tie exactly with the initial numbers collated at departure. Some of the units were reinforced in part thanks to the influx of sailors after Aboukir Bay. Likewise, the grenadiers of the 19th DB had begun to be dispatched to other units.

The Battle of Aboukir was fought on 25 July 1799, so ten days after the above return. It is therefore safe to assume that the numbers given had not changed too much. Bonaparte did not have at hand Kléber's division which formed the reserve and was still on its way.

Division Lanusse: 2,350
    32nd Line DB: 1,400
    18th Line DB: 950

Division Lannes: 3,900
    22nd Light DB: 1,100
    13th Line DB: 1,300
    69th Line DB: 1,500

Infantry battalions under the command of General Destaing: 1,800
    4th Light DB: 1 battalion, 300
    75th Line DB: 1 battalion, 500
    61st Line DB: 2 battalions, 1,000

Infantry total = 8,050

Guides under Bessières = 300

Cavalry under Murat = 1,000
    3rd Dragoons = 2 squadrons
    14th Dragoons = 2 squadrons
    7th *bis* Hussars = 2 squadrons

In addition there was some artillery, 100 dromedaries – the overall total tallies with the rough figure of 10,000 men given by Bonaparte after the event.

Losses were 100 killed and 500 wounded. Amongst the dead were Duvivier commander of the 14th Dragoons, Crétin who had become the new commander of the engineers after Cafarelli's death, Leturq, adjutant-general, and Guibert, ADC to Bonaparte and a nephew of the famous military theoretician who had so much inspired the young Bonaparte. Murat was also wounded as well as General Fugières and Chef de Brigade Morangier of the 18th Line DB. Although the victory was total and Turkish losses amounted to at least 6,000, the ferocity of the fighting, especially the cavalry shock, had taken its total. Murat had been shot through the jaw, and amazingly enough was to suffer no major consequences from such wound.

## The Army under Kléber and the Battle of Heliopolis

There are few army returns under Kléber's command which seem to have survived in the French archives unless they are hidden away in the general correspondence archival boxes. One document does give the state of the army on 25 September 1799, about a month after Kléber took command. It lists the units by branch indicating where they are and under which command.

Light Infantry
    2nd Light DB, 3 battalions: 1,231 in Salahieh
    4th Light DB, 3 battalions: 843 in Alexandria & Aboukir under Menou
    21st Light DB, 3 battalions: 1,412 in upper-Egypt under Desaix
    22nd Light DB, 3 battalions: 933, under Reynier
    Total light infantry: 4,419 men

Line Infantry
    9th Line DB, 3 battalions: 1,138 under Reynier
    13th Line DB, 3 battalions: 1,138 under Reynier
    18th Line DB, 3 battalions: 1,192, 2 battalions in Cairo, 1 in Rhamanie
    25th Line DB, 3 battalions: 1,202, 2 battalions under Dugua, 1 in Cairo
    32nd Line DB, 3 battalions: 1,239 in Damiette
    61st Line DB, 3 battalions: 1,030 under Dugua
    69th Line DB, 3 battalions: 1,117 under Menou
    75th Line DB, 3 battalions: 1,133 under Dugua
    85th Line DB, 3 battalions: 1,120 under Reynier
    88th Line DB, 3 battalions: 1,107 under Desaix
    Guides on foot: 59

Total line infantry = 11,475

Cavalry
   7th *bis* Hussars: 279 in Cairo with the general staff
   22nd Chasseurs: 329 in Boulak and Alexandria
   3rd Dragoons: 273 in Boulak
   14th Dragoons: 264 under Reynier
   15th Dragoons: 186 in Rosetta
   18th Dragoons: 189 in Damiette
   20th Dragoons: 356 in Boulak
   Mounted guides: 55
   Total cavalry = 1,931
   Dromedaries: 208

Engineers:
   Sappers: 670
   Miners: 82
   Workers: 60
   Balloon corps: 33

Artillery
   Foot Artillery: 1,064
   Light (mounted) Artillery: 357
   Artillery Train: 902
   Workers, & other artillery personnel: 445
   Total artillery: 2,768

The total return for the army indicates a strength of 21,646 men. This does yet not include legions or native troops.

   At the time of Heliopolis, Kléber's army was organised as follows:
   Commander in chief: Kléber, chief of staff: Damas
   Artillery: Songis
   Engineers: Sanson
   Guides: Deriot
   Dromedaries: Cavalier
   Mameluke Company: Hussein-Kachef

Division Reynier
   Brigade Robin: 22nd Light DB & 9th Line DB
   Brigade Lagrange: 13th Line DB, 85th Line DB, 25th Line DB
   Artillery: 1 11-pounder, 3 8-Pounders, 1 5-Pounder, 2 6-Pounder howitzers.

Division Friant
   Brigade Belliard: 21st Light DB, 61st Line DB
   Brigade Donzelot: 75th Line DB, 88th Line DB

# LINING UP THE TROOPS: ORDERS OF BATTLE OF THE ARMY OF THE ORIENT 1798-1802

Artillery: 1 11-Pounder, 2 8-Pounders, 1 5-Pounder, 2 6-Pounder howitzers

Cavalry under Leclerc d'Ostein
 7th *bis* Hussars
 22nd Chasseurs
 3rd Dragoons
 14th Dragoons
 Artillery: 4 8-pounders plus 2 howitzers

In total French forces at Heliopolis were around 10,000 men. Again this was a major victory as Ottoman forces lost about 9,000 men. French losses amounted to only 450, mainly wounded.

The grand attack on Cairo at the time of the second insurrection claimed only 10 killed and some 60 wounded on the French side versus a loss of about 2,000 killed and countless wounded on the Turkish-Egyptian side.

## Situation of the Army Prior to the British Landing at Alexandria, 21 January 1801

Under Menou, given the relative lack of military activity and his own obsession with controlling everything, we have quite a few returns. Just prior to the British landing, there is a complete listing of all units.

| Branch | Unit | General officers & staff | Officers | Men fit for Duty | Men in hospital | Total Fit for Duty | Grand Total | Officers' Horses | Men's Horses | Artillery Horses | Camels |
|---|---|---|---|---|---|---|---|---|---|---|---|
| Light Infantry | 2nd Light DB | | 79 | 807 | 54 | 886 | 940 | 21 | | 13 | 8 |
| | 4th Light DB | | 74 | 860 | 69 | 934 | 1,003 | 17 | | 14 | 9 |
| | 21st Light DB | | 83 | 1,645 | 100 | 1,728 | 1,828 | 20 | | 13 | 36 |
| | 22nd Light DB | | 69 | 871 | 31 | 940 | 971 | 28 | | 9 | 17 |
| Line Infantry | 9th Line DB | | 76 | 979 | 20 | 1,055 | 1,075 | 43 | | 9 | 16 |
| | 13th Line DB | | 66 | 994 | 19 | 1,060 | 1,079 | 29 | | 12 | 17 |
| | 18th Line DB | | 65 | 905 | 82 | 970 | 1,052 | 28 | | 13 | 9 |
| | 25th Line DB | | 95 | 1,055 | 146 | 1,150 | 1,296 | 20 | | 15 | 10 |
| | 32nd Line DB | | 75 | 1,152 | 21 | 1,227 | 1,248 | 20 | | 14 | 11 |
| | 61st Line DB | | 70 | 1,134 | 32 | 1,204 | 1,236 | 21 | | 11 | 9 |
| | 69th Line DB | | 69 | 941 | 33 | 1,010 | 1,043 | 19 | | 15 | 10 |
| | 75th Line DB | | 77 | 1,049 | 13 | 1,126 | 1,139 | 20 | | 14 | 11 |
| | 85th Line DB | | 69 | 1,018 | 37 | 1,087 | 1,124 | 27 | | 13 | 16 |
| | 88th Line DB | | 78 | 990 | 38 | 1,068 | 1,106 | 24 | | 13 | 14 |
| Invalids | Invalid DB | | 49 | 784 | 44 | 833 | 877 | | | | |

# THE FRENCH ARMY OF THE ORIENT 1798–1801

| Branch | Unit | General officers & staff | Officers | Men fit for Duty | Men in hospital | Total Fit for Duty | Grand Total | Officers' Horses | Men's Horses | Artillery Horses | Camels |
|---|---|---|---|---|---|---|---|---|---|---|---|
| Guides | Foot & Mounted | | 16 | 269 | 13 | 285 | 298 | 40 | 73 | 63 | 6 |
| Cavalry | Dromedaries | | 24 | 306 | 6 | 330 | 336 | 27 | | | 273 |
| | 7th *bis* Hussars | | 36 | 281 | 4 | 317 | 321 | 86 | 251 | | 5 |
| | 22nd Chasseurs | | 39 | 277 | 7 | 316 | 323 | 81 | 184 | | 7 |
| | 3rd Dragoons | | 37 | 254 | 8 | 291 | 299 | 82 | 225 | | 6 |
| | 14th Dragoons | | 34 | 314 | 6 | 348 | 354 | 80 | 276 | | 6 |
| | 15th Dragoons | | 30 | 185 | 5 | 215 | 220 | 72 | 129 | | 5 |
| | 18th Dragoons | | 31 | 173 | 8 | 204 | 212 | 71 | 90 | | 7 |
| | 20th Dragoons | | 33 | 298 | 3 | 331 | 334 | 39 | 160 | | 8 |
| | Horse Depot | | 4 | 10 | 0 | 14 | 14 | 5 | 63 | | 16 |
| Artillery | Staff | 18 | 14 | 32 | | 64 | 64 | 68 | | | 14 |
| | 4th Regiment | | 46 | 616 | 13 | 662 | 675 | 21 | | | |
| | Light Artillery Squadron | | 19 | 276 | 6 | 295 | 301 | 31 | 245 | | |
| | Train | | 11 | 1,037 | 25 | 1,048 | 1,073 | | | 1,183 | 602 |
| | Workers | | 11 | 211 | 6 | 222 | 228 | 3 | | | |
| | Pontoon | | 4 | 71 | 3 | 75 | 78 | | | | |
| | Gunsmiths | | 4 | 69 | 5 | 73 | 78 | 1 | | | |
| | Explosive Specialists | | 3 | 28 | 1 | 31 | 32 | | | | |
| | Navy | | 16 | 278 | 7 | 294 | 301 | 10 | | | |
| | Guards | | | 113 | 4 | 113 | 117 | | | | |
| | Copt Workers | | 3 | 94 | 3 | 97 | 100 | | | | |
| Engineers | Staff | 2 | 33 | 5 | | 40 | 40 | 85 | | | |
| | Sappers | | 25 | 491 | 11 | 516 | 527 | 9 | | | 4 |
| | Miners | | 7 | 64 | 2 | 71 | 73 | 6 | | | |
| | Workers | | 4 | 57 | | 61 | 61 | 10 | | | |
| | Balloon Corps | | 4 | 25 | | 29 | 29 | 6 | | | |
| | Civilian Workers | | | 40 | | 40 | 40 | | | | |
| Headquarters | General Staff | 112 | 5 | | | 117 | 117 | 180 | | | 80 |
| | Forts & Strongholds Staff | | 40 | | | 40 | 40 | 48 | | | 34 |
| Review Inspectors | | | 1 | | | 1 | 1 | 6 | | | 5 |
| War Commissary | | | 1 | 21 | | 22 | 22 | 36 | | | 38 |
| Arts & Science commission | | | 38 | | | 38 | 38 | 29 | | | |

# LINING UP THE TROOPS: ORDERS OF BATTLE OF THE ARMY OF THE ORIENT 1798-1802

| Branch | Unit | General officers & staff | Officers | Men fit for Duty | Men in hospital | Total Fit for Duty | Grand Total | Officers' Horses | Men's Horses | Artillery Horses | Camels |
|---|---|---|---|---|---|---|---|---|---|---|---|
| Staff Engineers | Topographic Engineers | | 10 | | | 10 | 10 | 13 | | | |
| | Civil Work Engineers | | 18 | | | 18 | 18 | 19 | | | |
| Medical Services | Doctors | | 15 | | | 15 | 15 | 15 | | | |
| | Surgeons | | 51 | | | 51 | 51 | 39 | | | |
| | Pharmacists | | 41 | | | 41 | 41 | 16 | | | |
| Administration | Supplies | | | 221 | | 221 | 221 | | | | |
| | Hospitals | | | 38 | | 38 | 38 | | | | |
| | Field Hospitals | | | 41 | | 41 | 41 | | | | |
| | Public Treasury | | | 27 | | 27 | 27 | | | | |
| | Printing House | | | 17 | | 17 | 17 | | | | |
| | Reserve Train | | | 31 | | 31 | 31 | | | | |
| | Mint | | | 6 | | 6 | 6 | | | | |
| Legions | Syrian | | 10 | 266 | | 276 | 276 | 27 | 177 | | |
| | Greek | | 21 | 346 | 12 | 367 | 379 | | | | |
| | Copt | | 23 | 684 | 9 | 707 | 716 | | | | |
| | Janissaries | | 2 | 80 | | 82 | 82 | | | | |
| Total | | 134 | 1,877 | 22,815 | 906 | 24,547 | 25,453 | 1,598 | 1,873 | 1,424 | 1,309 |

As can be seen the army looks on paper to be still an effective and important fighting force. The number of men fit for duty, 22,000 is almost identical to that available in the summer of 1798. However, one cannot really compare the two forces. Aside from the 'legions' which represent less than 2,000 men or ten per cent of the force, almost all units had been reinforced with 'native' recruitment. The 21st Light Demi-Brigade, especially, has in its ranks Egyptians and many former slaves from Darfur who have been very officially purchased to join the army. Likewise Maltese and Copts had been pressed into the service of various units. Finally, all young able-bodied young French civilians had also been transferred from civilian duties into the military. Thus, combined with the lack of military activity, the army which was about to face the British was far less well trained and effective than the initial force that had just come from two years of campaigning in Italy.

## French forces at the Battle of Alexandria (Canope) 21 March 1801

The best source for the French order of battle remains Reynier's own account of the fight.

# THE FRENCH ARMY OF THE ORIENT 1798–1801

Commander in chief: Général de Division Abdallah Jacques Menou

A. Infantry

i) Right Wing under Général de Division Reynier
    3,450 men
    9 four-pounders
    6 eight-pounders
    3 howitzers

    Général de Division Damas: 1,700 men
    Général de Brigade Baudot
        13th Line DB: 840 men
        2 four-pounders
        3 eight-pounders
        1 howitzer
        85th Line DB: 860 men
        2 four-pounders

    Général de Division Friant: 1,750 men
    Général de Brigade Délegorgue
        25th Line DB: 650 men
        2 four-pounders
        3 eight-pounders
        2 howitzers
        61st Line DB: 500 men
        2 four-pounders
        75th Line DB: 600 men
        1 four-pounder

ii) Centre under Général de Division Rampon
    2,030 men
    3 four-pounders
    Chef de Brigade Eppler (commander 21st Light DB)
        Greek Grenadiers: 100 men
        25th Line DB, 2 grenadier companies: 120 men
        21st Light DB, 1 carabinier company: 80 men
    Général de Brigade Destaing
        21st Light DB: 1st & 2nd battalions: 700 men
        1 four-pounder
    Adjutant-Commandant Sornet
        2nd Light DB: Carabiniers: 180 men
        32nd Line DB: Grenadiers: 150 men
        32nd Line DB: 700 men
        2 four-pounders

iii) Left Wing under Général de Division Lanusse
    2,850 men

# LINING UP THE TROOPS: ORDERS OF BATTLE OF THE ARMY OF THE ORIENT 1798-1802

8 four-pounders
6 eight-pounders
3 twelve-pounders
3 howitzers
Général de Brigade Silly
    4th Light DB: 600 men
    2 four-pounders
    4 eight-pounders
    2 howitzers
    18e Line DB: 600 men
    2 four-pounders
Général de Brigade Valentin
    69th Line DB: 800 men
    2 four-pounders
    88th Line DB: 700 men
    2 four-pounders

Guides on foot & guides artillery: 150 men
2 eight-pounders
1 howitzer

Artillery reserve: 3 twelve-pounders
Sappers: 50 men

B. Cavalry: under the command of Général de Brigade Roize

i) Cavalry Reserve
    900 men
    4 eight-pounders
    2 howitzers
    Général de Brigade Boussart
        3rd Dragoons: 200 men
        14th Dragoons: 250 men
    Général de Brigade Roize
        15th Dragoons: 150 men
        18th Dragoons: 100 men
        20th Dragoons: 200 men

ii) Cavalry on the right wing (detached)
    350 men
    Général de Brigade Bron
        7th *bis* Hussars: 200 men
        22nd Chasseurs: 150 men

Coptic Legion by Eugene Lami. The Coptic Legion was a late creation. Interestingly, this plate seems like a good rendering of the uniform worn; a green yellow-faced short coat. In this specific case, head-dress and epaulettes are consistent with a grenadier.

C. Dromedaries: Chef d'Escadron Cavalier: 130 men

D. Summary
   Right Wing: 3,450 men, 18 guns
   Centre: 2,030 men, 3 guns
   Left Wing: 2,700 men, 14 guns
   Guides, Artillery, Sappers: 150 men, 6 guns
   Cavalry Reserve: 900 men, 6 guns
   Right Wing Cavalry: 350 men
   Dromedaries: 130 men
   In total: 9710 men, 47 guns

The composition of the force breaks down as follows: 8,330 foot soldiers (86 per cent), 1,250 cavalrymen (13 per cent), 130 dromedaries (1 per cent)

Artillery by Calibre
   21 four-pounders (44 per cent)
   16 eight-pounders (33 per cent)
   3 twelve-pounders (6 per cent)
   8 howitzers (17 per cent)

At the start of the campaign, Menou lined up 13,372 infantrymen and 1,661 cavalrymen for a total of 15,033 men. In addition 6,294 men were at their regimental depot, on garrison, on the Nile flotilla etc. 477 cavalrymen were dismounted due to lack of horses; 348 gunners were on fortress duty. This gives a total of 22,152 men, so quite close to that of the January return when excluding administrative services. Out of the total army available for active operations, Menou brought to Alexandria 62 per cent of his infantry and 75 per cent of his cavalry.

## Belliard's Forces in Cairo

While Menou was shutting himself up in Alexandria after his defeat, Belliard was being besieged in Cairo. He had the rest of the Army of the Orient with him. The French war archives hold a detailed return dated 22 July 1801, a month after the surrender of Cairo and just prior to boarding ships back to France. The figures given below are only the men fit for duty.

Staff & administration:
General Staff: 32 officers
   1 Général de Division, commander-in-chief
   2 Généraux de Division
   7 Généraux de Brigade
   4 Adjutant-Commanders
   18 ADCs
   War Commissary: 9 Commissaries and 2 aides
   Geographical Engineers: 5
   Civil Works Engineers: 4 and 2 aides
   Total staff and administration = 54

# LINING UP THE TROOPS: ORDERS OF BATTLE OF THE ARMY OF THE ORIENT 1798-1802

Artillery:
- Staff & Artillery Park: 43 officers, 35 men
- Light Artillery, 3rd squadron: 12 officers, 155 men
- 4th Artillery: 14 officers, 169 men
- Copt, Greek artillery, 12th company of Fortress Artillery: 7 officers, 199 men
- Naval Artillery: 9 officers, 152 men
- Pontoon & Explosive Specialists: 11 officers, 172 men
- Artillery Train: 2 officers, 318 men
- Total artillery = 1,298

Engineers:
- Staff: 14 officers, 5 men
- Miners: 2 officers, 30 men
- Workers: 5 officers, 72 men
- Sappers: 12 officers, 212 men
- Total engineers = 352

Guides: 2 officers and 29 men
- Total guides = 31

Dromedaries: 10 officers, 155 men
- Total dromedaries = 165

Cavalry:
- 7th *bis* Hussars: 32 officers, 235 men
- 22nd Chasseurs: 33 officers, 215 men
- 3rd Dragoons: 14 officers, 147 men
- 14th Dragoons: 9 officers, 106 men
- 15th Dragoons: 17 officers, 135 men
- 20th Dragoons: 26 officers, 186 men
- 1st Regiment of Mamelukes: 12 officers, 233 men
- Mounted Copts: 3 officers, 57 men
- Total cavalry = 1,460

Infantry:
- 2nd Light Demi-Brigade: 46 officers, 474 men
- 4th Light Demi-Brigade: 51 officers, 602 men
- 21st Light Demi-Brigade: 46 officers, 831 men
- 22nd Light Demi-Brigade: 64 officers, 715 men
- 9th Line Demi-Brigade: 66 officers, 829 men
- 13th Line Demi-Brigade: 59 officers, 819 men
- 69th Line Demi-Brigade: 58 officers, 620 men
- 85th Line Demi-Brigade: 62 officers, 756 men

Greek Legion by Eugene Lami. Another late levy. The men wore their national dress, although it seems officers wore a French-style dress (see background). Like the Coptic Legion, this plate inspired many artists who later depicted these units (such as Valmont, Boisselier etc.).

Regimental depots
  18th Line Demi-Brigade: 7 officers, 117 men
  25th Line Demi-Brigade: 10 officers, 24 men
  32nd Line Demi-Brigade: 9 officers, 45 men
  75th Line Demi-Brigade: 3 officers, 14 men
  88th Line Demi-Brigade: 12 officers, 175 men

Invalids: 29 officers, 381 men

Coptic Legion: 23 officers, 286 men

Greek Legion: 20 officers, 204 men

Naval troops: 36 officers, 286 men (includes officers without troops, naval administration)

  Total infantry = 7,779

Science & Arts Commission: 8
Balloon Corps: 26
Mathematics School: 35
Printing Office: 1
Doctors: 9
Surgeons: 32
Pharmacists: 27

Grand total = 11,277 men fit for duty

  A few comments:
  This return clearly mentions the 1st Regiment of Mamelukes, which is the ancestor of the future Consular Guard and then Imperial Guard Mamelukes.
  Copts and Greeks are not only serving as infantry, but there is also artillery and cavalry for Copts and artillery for Greeks.
  The mathematics school was an institution set up for young men civilian or military (especially navy) to ensure their continued training.
  There were just another 530 men in hospital or unfit for duty.
  There were another 1,079 individuals 'following the army' – women, servants etc. – which brings the full total to just under 13,000 people. It is interesting to note that this breakdown actually assumes that servants are men only. Also both of these categories are further broken down into 'French', 'from the land', and 'black' (i.e. from southern Egypt or elsewhere in Africa). There were still 166 French women by then, with 124 Egyptians and 107 Africans.

5

# Uniforms – 'The Most Beautiful Sight the Eye Could Behold'[1]

More than any other army of the period, the French forces in Egypt underwent considerable and multiple changes in their uniforms and equipment. Logistical constraints, climate, and fighting conditions all explain this. Whereas some innovations in organisation or equipment were later implemented in the French army, the radical changes in uniforms were as quickly set aside as they had been adopted. Actually, this aspect of the French soldier in Egypt was completely forgotten and it is only after more than a hundred years of detective work that we can piece together a reasonable picture of what those men looked like when they marched into Syria, or fought at Heliopolis and Alexandria. The history of dress of the Army of Orient dress can be divided into three main periods:

- The regulation 'European' dress worn until the end of 1798.
- The cotton uniforms, adopted as of end of 1798 until the end of 1799.
- The so-called 'Kléber' uniforms worn from the autumn of 1799 until the departure from Egypt.

To this, one must also add the uniforms worn by the newly created units: Nautical Legion, Dromedaries, Coptic Legion, Greek Legion, et cetera, all of which we will treat independently from the study of the main body of the army.

**The European Uniforms**
The troops that sailed out to Egypt in the spring of 1798 wore the same dress they had worn in Italy over the past two years of campaigning. Those were the standard uniforms worn by the French Revolutionary army. We shall call them 'regulation' although the term is somewhat inappropriate.

In 1786, an exhaustive set of dress regulations had been issued by the royal government. These were somewhat modified in 1791, with the most conspicuous change being the adoption for infantry and mounted chasseurs of a Tarleton style helmet. Odd as it may seem, the next complete regulations

---
1  Quoting Grandjean, head of the clothing department of the Army of the Orient.

# THE FRENCH ARMY OF THE ORIENT 1798–1801

Sucy by Dutertre. It is only apt that we show what the two main head commissioners (ordonnateurs) in charge of the army looked like. Sucy was an ageing man who quickly felt overwhelmed by the task at hand. Suffering from a major wound, he took that excuse to go back to France, which Bonaparte had no problems in granting him. Unfortunately, captured on the shores of the kingdom of Naples, Sucy was to die at the hands of the local population there.

were to be issued only in 1812! In practice, many small and large changes were made either officially, such as going from white to blue for infantry coats, or out of fashion insofar as changes to the cut for coats was concerned. To all this, one must add that the French Revolutionary army lived very much off the land it occupied and would present if not a ragged look, then at least a fairly motley aspect!

It does seem, however, that the troops which embarked for Egypt had been well provided-for and had new clothing and equipment. We have several letters from Bonaparte to some of his generals, like Desaix, insisting on such aspects. Let us therefore describe what the troops wore as they attacked Malta and then landed at Alexandria and fought at the Pyramids.

### Staff

Initially after the Revolution there were not many changes in the uniforms worn by generals and their staffs. In 1791, the breeches and waistcoat which had traditionally been red became white. Then in 1794, the uniform was more closely regulated. A coat of 'national blue' with a large turned-down red collar, and red cuffs. One rank of a large ribbon was to distinguish the généraux de brigade, a second rank of a thinner ribbon was to be added for généraux de division. Unfortunately, the term 'ribbon' is all but enough of a description. It seems that the lace design of this 'ribbon' was similar to what had been in use since the monarchy, that is flowing circular style patterns. In 1796, further specifications were added:

- A general-in-chief was to wear a red and white sash with a gold braid ending and have red plumes on his hat with a central tricolour plume. His coat was to be laced extensively.
- A général de division was to have an all red sash with a tricolour braiding, with dark red plumes topped by a tricolour plume on the hat. Double lace only on his collar, cuffs, and pockets
- A général de brigade, light blue sash ended in tricolour braiding, with tricolour plumes topped by a tricolour plume. Same lace pattern as the général de division but a single lace.

As for ADCs they wore a coat of similar cut, but with a sky blue collar and having an arm band on the left arm similar to the sash of the general to which they were attached. It was this regulation which applied when the army set out for Egypt.

However on 7 August 1798, the regulation changed and for the first time detailed plates were provided with it. The biggest change was the adoption of a lace featuring for the first time in French military history the oak leaves pattern. There were also some changes on the plumes. The general-in-chief was to have three red plumes at the base and a light white plume with a blue base; the général de division, three red plumes with a white and blue plume; for the général de brigade, three blue plumes with a red and white plume in the centre. The other major change was that ADCs were now to keep wearing their regimental uniforms but with the armband on the left arm as previously indicated and were to have a plume which was tricolour at the base but with a yellow tip. These new regulations were probably quickly implemented, as it is quite possible the oak leaves pattern had already been in unofficial use. So we can assume that this was the case as of the early autumn of 1798.

Guides

The Guides of the Army of Italy, who became the Guides of the Army of the Orient, wore a regulation coat of dark green with pointed cuffs and lapels; red collar, cuffs, and turnbacks; green lapels piped red. They had a red waistcoat, wore a hat and Hungarian breeches. Mounted guides had hussar style boots and equipment, foot guides had ankle length gaiters. This was the uniform which was later to be adopted by the Chasseurs of the Consular Guard as undress uniform. Very soon after the entrance into Cairo, luxury weapons that had been captured form the Mamelukes, specifically gold or silver ornamented blunderbusses, were issued to the Guides officers and NCOs. Presumably the same was true for sabres, saddles etc.

Line Infantry

The general aspect of the French revolutionary infantryman is well known and was not to change massively until 1806 with the adoption of the so-called Napoleonic shako. In 1798, the dress worn was strictly in accordance with the 1786 regulation.

Coat: Known as 'habit à la française' literally 'French coat', it opened up on the front in a distinctive 18th century style with lapels ending up at the top in a 'butterfly' design.
   The cut of the coat was fairly loose. Coat tail lapels were also not sewn or 'fake' as later during the empire, but were effectively 'turned back' and attached. After the Republic had replaced the monarchy and with the merging of the old royalist units with the National Guard and volunteer troops, the regimental colour distinctions were abandoned as were the old coat colours (white for French troops, blue for German and Italians, red for Irish or Swiss). The coat became a universal dark blue, known as 'bleu national' (national blue). The blue used was later to be known as 'imperial blue', and much later, 'royal blue', becoming the most politically neutral colour of that period!
   It had white lapels piped red, red collar and cuffs piped white (or not), with cuff flaps which could be red, white, or blue and piped (or not) in red or white. The coat tails were white, which was logical as the coat lining was of that colour and could be piped red or not. Back tail pockets were vertical and usually piped red. There were no strict rules as for piping, likewise for cuff flaps which were sometimes completely absent. Fusilier coats had a simple blue shoulder strap, piped red. Grenadiers had red

# THE FRENCH ARMY OF THE ORIENT 1798–1801

Hector Daure by Dutertre. The youthful and brilliant Daure was actually the man who brilliantly managed all the supplies of the army and was ultimately responsible for its clothing and equipment. His personal papers which are now in the French war archives are an essential source for anyone researching the Army of the Orient

wool epaulettes. Buttons were round and of yellow metal with variable patterns, typically having the number of the regiment.

The cloth used for the coat was wool. For rank and file, as well as NCOs, it would be of rather coarse quality. For officers, the cloth would be much finer.

Waistcoat: Under the coat, the men would wear a simple white waistcoat which would be visible given the open cut of the coat. Buttons would be of yellow metal or wood covered with white cloth. Out of fantasy or lack of supply, some men could wear red waistcoats. Like the coat, the waistcoat could be of woollen cloth or more rarely linen.

Breeches: French infantry would wear white breeches, again of rather coarse woollen cloth. During some earlier Revolutionary campaigns, men had sometimes worn trousers made from bedsheets, mattress cloth, or any material they could find. It is quite clear that as they embarked into Egypt, breeches were worn, as indeed the change from breeches to trousers was very specifically stated at the end of 1798.

Gaiters: Men wore either white or dark grey gaiters with buttons on the side (again yellow metal or wood covered with cloth). Dark gaiters were usually worn on campaign, while white were reserved for summer wearing or full dress. The gaiters for line infantry would go above knee level.

Shoes: Soldiers wore simple leather shoes of average to mediocre quality. There was a constant need of supply for these as they were essential. Contrarily to popular belief and based on surviving sets, the shoes were true pairs, left and right. Officers wore boots reaching to just below knee level, typically black with a yellowish-tan upper part just below the knee.

Headdress: Was the 1791 helmet still in use in the regiments that went out to Egypt ? We actually do not know and, as we will see when discussing the special Egyptian cap adopted, it is probable some of these Tarleton style helmets were present. In any case, this helmet had not proven very popular. The very few rank and file versions that have survived to this day are actually quite ugly in appearance. The officer versions are only marginally better-looking! It also seems to have been heavy and cumbersome to wear. The most common headdress was the hat, which was actually a three cornered hat with the front corner being much less pronounced, giving it an almost two-cornered look. It had a tricolour cockade held in place by silk bands and a regimental button. A small coloured tuft would crown it. The cockade design was not set, the only guidance was that it had to show the three national colours: red, white, and blue.

Bearskin caps with a frontal yellow-metal plate were sometimes worn by grenadiers, but it all depended on availability of supplies. More commonly, grenadiers would wear a hat and be identified by a red carrot-shaped tuft of a larger size than that of the fusiliers, or a drooping red plume. Sappers would wear a bearskin, but with no metal plate.

Officers would wear the same hat or bearskin as their men, but it would have gold lace to hold the cockade and be overall of a better quality.

Equipment: Fusiliers would have only one shoulder belt passing over the left shoulder and supporting both the large black cartridge box and the bayonet. Grenadiers and NCOs would wear crossed shoulder belts. The left shoulder belt would have just the cartridge box, the right one would hold a small model 1767 infantry sabre and the bayonet. NCO ranks were indicated on one or both sleeves: 2 yellow angled stripes, would denote a corporal; one similar but gold above red cloth, a sergeant; and two gold above red, a sergeant major. The haversack was a simple one made out of brown cow skin.

Weapons: The regulation musket was the 1777 Gribeauval musket which had been introduced as part of the overall Gribeauval system. It was later to be slightly modified in 1800 (Year IX) to become the '1777 Modifié AN IX' which was the standard weapon of the Napoleonic wars. The older version held the muzzle cap with a small screw which would tend to break and it was replaced by a spring. Sturdy, heavy but reliable, it was a real improvement over previous French models. Given the massive needs for weapons during the Revolution, multiple factories had turned out all kinds of muskets, sometimes pressing back into service some older models, or using older spare parts. Some of these were probably to be found in Egypt.

The regulation sabre was the 1767 'briquet'. Its style was very much of the 18th century and was to be replaced, again in 1800, by a new simplified version with a rounder hilt. Fusilier officers would carry a straight sword, while grenadier officers a curved sabre.

Officers would also usually carry pistols. As they were usually dismounted, those pistols would be short ones held in their coat pockets. A typical pair would be the short 'gendarmerie' model which was regulation issue to the gendarme units. Alternatively, short civilian versions would be used. In theory, officers and NCOs could be equipped with the 1793 short infantry rifle manufactured in Versailles. This rifle, although a beautiful piece of craftsmanship, had proven cumbersome to use and was not at all popular. The need for a long arm in Egypt across all ranks became however quickly obvious.

From the above description, there are two observations to be made:

The coat cut and woollen cloth were acceptable in a European climate. Let us remember that the end of the 18th and early 19th century were subject to what has been called a 'little ice age'. However, the heavy cloth and uncomfortable cut made the uniforms a true nuisance. In addition the harsh early campaigning took quickly its toll on the uniforms which were in shreds by the early autumn.

There were no overcoats! This was not part of any regulation and was not be a standard issue until 1806 after the cold 1805 Austerlitz campaign. As is well known, night time in the desert tends to be very cold and so there was an urgent need to supply such an item to infantry.

Light Infantry
Light infantry demi-brigades were a recent innovation and had been born out of the foot components of the old legions of chasseurs. Initially clothed in green, they had switched over to an all dark blue outfit.

Coat: From the front it seemed similar in cut to the line infantry coat, but its coat tails were actually shorter. It was all dark blue, piped in white including the collar for chasseurs (the light infantry equivalent of fusiliers). Cuffs, however, were pointed and piped white in typical 'light branch of service' fashion. Carabiniers (equivalent of grenadiers) would have a red collar piped white.

Waistcoat and breeches: similar to line infantry but usually dark blue, although white waistcoats could be worn.

Gaiters: short dark grey gaiters or none.

Headdress: similar hat as line infantry but with a green tuft or green drooping plume, otherwise carabiniers wore drooping red plum or tuft.

All yellow metal (buttons etc.) for the line troops was white metal for the light infantry. Weapons were identical to line infantry, although shorter muskets (typically dragoon models) would be issued wherever possible. Officers all carried sabres and no straight swords.

Cavalry
French cavalry had undergone much less changes in uniforms because of the Revolution than the infantry. Its aspect was still very much that of 1786 or 1791, with the exception that new units had been raised, and that of course the tricolour cockade had replaced the white.

Dragoons
Dragoons were initially mounted infantry and so logically they wore the same coat as the line infantry with square lapels and cuffs with flaps. Regiments were distinguished by colour combinations on collar, lapels, cuffs, cuff flaps and type of pockets. Dragoons wore a brass helmet with a flowing horse-hair mane. The helmet style was that of the 1786 regulation. They wore white or cream coloured breeches with either heavy cavalry boots or smaller ones. On campaign, dragoons like the rest of the cavalry would wear cavalry overalls over their breeches to protect them. These were dark green with a large piping in the distinctive colour running down the side with brass buttons. The inside of the overalls was reinforced with dark leather, black or brown.

They were armed with a specific dragoon musket, slightly shorter than the regular line infantry musket and with a reinforced iron band at mid-barrel so that it can safely be slung across the body with no risk of breaking. Their sabre had a straight blade with a brass pommel.

Regimental distinctions for the dragoon regiments of the Army of the Orient were as follows:

- 3rd Dragoons: scarlet collar, lapels, turnbacks, and cuff flaps; horizontal pockets piped scarlet; cuffs piped scarlet.
- 14th Dragoons: pink lapels, turnbacks and cuffs; horizontal pockets piped pink; cuff flaps piped pink
- 15th Dragoons: pink collar, lapels, turnbacks, and cuff flaps; horizontal pockets piped pink; cuffs piped pink.
- 18th Dragoons: pink collar, lapels, turnbacks and cuff flaps; vertical pockets piped pink; cuffs piped pink.
- 20th Dragoons: yellow lapels, turnbacks, and cuffs; horizontal pockets piped yellow; cuff flaps piped yellow.

The pink colour was fairly dark, while yellow should have been a bright light yellow, but was often a faded tint almost cream.

As for saddles, initially two dark green holster caps piped with the distinctive colour were worn, but replaced in 1791 by a sheepskin shabrack with dragon's teeth of the distinctive colour. This was not always applied and both may have existed in Egypt. The saddlecloth was dark green piped with the distinctive colour.

Trumpeters would typically have worn the same outfit as the troop but with the colours inverted, i.e. a coat of the distinctive colour faced green, and they would be mounted on light grey horses. The helmet horsehair mane could be white or alternatively they would wear a hat.

### 7th *bis* Hussars

This unit had started as a Parisian volunteer corps called the 'Hussards de la Liberté'. Its uniform therefore featured the colours of the city of Paris, red and blue. It normally had a blue dolman braided yellow, a red pelisse also braided yellow, and red Hungarian breeches. On campaign the breeches were protected by dark blue cavalry overalls with a red band and black bone buttons. As a headdress it wore initially the mirliton shako looking very much like a truncated cone. Made of black felt or leather, it had a red flame with blue back circling it. In effect the shako looked more red than black. We have no concrete evidence for the plume colour(s) if worn – entirely black or black with a red tip seem the most logical. We know of a specific model for the 7th *bis* which was probably used also in Egypt. All black leather with a large cursive B with a 7 within the bottom part of the B.

The troopers of the 7th *bis* Hussars were armed with the curved Hungarian style sabre. Many variations of make existed during the Revolution. Hilts and fittings should have been brass, but in some cases, fittings were made of iron.. Hussars also carried in theory the 1786 model hussar musketoon. Again multiple versions existed using iron rather than brass fittings.

The saddle was covered by a sheepskin shabrack with blue dragon's teeth.

The 7th *bis* Hussars' trumpeters wore a distinctive all-red uniform consisting of a coat with no lapels, but with a blue collar, cuffs, turnbacks and pipings. Red breeches piped blue on the side and a hat instead of a mirliton.

### 22nd Chasseurs

In 1791, the chasseurs wore the regular 1786 infantry coat, dark green with the 1791 infantry Tarleton-style helmet. There were then only twelve chasseurs regiments. Their number quickly inflated given the influx of volunteer units which were converted into regular chasseur regiments. Most of these units had adopted hussar-style uniforms and so, quite logically, the chasseurs mimicked the hussars to some degree. Typically a green dolman braided white was adopted with collar and cuffs of the facing colour. Pelisses were also worn in some cases. In some cases also a sabretache was worn. The 1791 helmet, unanimously disliked especially by cavalry, was discarded and replaced by the hussar mirliton shako.

The 22nd Chasseurs adopted almost the full hussar uniform. Green dolman, pelisse, and breeches. The distinctive colour was 'capucine' which is a bright orange and, under the dolman, chasseurs would have a light orange waistcoat. The headdress was similar to that of the hussars, but the flame was of course light orange. Again, dark green cavalry overalls would be worn on campaign.

Sabretaches were worn by officers; horse equipment and armament were similar to the hussars.

Trumpeters wore a style of uniform similar to those of the 7th *bis* Hussars, but the coat was light orange faced green and the breeches were green.

### Foot Artillery

The foot artillery wore the same uniform as the infantry except that it was all blue with red piping at the lapels, collar, cuff flaps, and pockets. Cuffs and turnbacks were red. A red falling plume could be worn on top of the hat.

### Light Artillery

Light artillery followed light cavalry fashion and there were no strict regulations. Images of the period show this branch of the service wearing regulation coats with pointed red cuffs and pointed lapels piped red. Turnbacks would be red. A mirliton shako with blue flame piped red would be worn, or sometimes a dragoon style leather helmet. Horse equipment was similar to that of hussars and chasseurs.

### Engineers

The engineering branch wore the same uniform as the artillery except that collar, lapels, and cuffs were black and of black velvet for officers.

### Balloon Corps

Although part of engineers, the balloon corps had adopted a visually different uniform. Instead of blue the coat was green but otherwise had the black of the engineers on cuffs, cuff flaps, and lapels.

## The Cotton Uniform and the Advent of the Egyptian 'Tufted Cap'

On 28 July 1798, so barely three days after entering Cairo, Bonaparte ordered the formation of a 'clothing council' for the army, bringing together delegate officers from each infantry division, cavalry brigade, artillery' and engineers.

They were to meet on 30 July at noon at Ordonnateur Sucy's house along with the clothing agent for the army. They were to 'work without delay on this most important matter according to the details and execution instructions sent by the commander in chief'.

Unlike some general officers of the period who have gone down in history as taking excellent care of the welfare of his troops (like Kléber, or 'Daddy' Hill in Britain), Napoleon Bonaparte does not have such reputation. He actually had a very utilitarian view of his men. They were a means to a strategic end. As a tool, the army had to be maintained in an adequate fighting condition. The importance of providing an ample re-supply of shoes is something which constantly comes back in his correspondence right up to 1815. The creation of this clothing council is to be understood in such a context. The army had landed with its European uniform. It had of course, proven far too hot during the day and not protective enough for cold desert nights. Several accounts state that for many men, their uniform was in tatters: perspiration, sand and just the long desert haul had transformed the smart uniforms into rags. The matter had indeed become urgent for any further campaigning to be done.

One will note that the council was not to debate the clothing to be worn by the army. Such a decision would have already been made by Bonaparte. All there was to discuss is how and when the new clothing will be implemented.

Unfortunately for us, Sucy's papers have not survived. He probably carried the originals with him back to France and they were lost when he was captured on the Neapolitan coast. Any copies which may perhaps have existed have not surfaced. We do however have the daily orders which spell out the final decisions to some (limited) details and more importantly tailor-in-chief Bernoyer's letters.

In a letter to his wife written on the 30 July, Bernoyer indicates:

> On the 26th, Bonaparte had me called. He asked me to quickly design different uniform models for the troops so he could choose one which would be best suited to the land and its climate. He advised me to avoid any constraint in the clothing of the soldiers. Amongst the various models I presented to him the next day, the following was chosen: A rather loose coat with turnbacks and buttoned down to the waist so as to get rid of the waistcoat, trousers made of cotton and ending up with half-gaiters such that the shoes would be well covered and the sand would not get into them during desert journeys.

Upon this Bonaparte asked him how long it would take to cloth ten thousand men. Bernoyer came back the following day (28 July) at dawn indicating this could be done within thirty-five days. It was on that very day that Bonaparte, now having all the pieces in his hand, issued the order instituting the clothing council. All that remained therefore was to spell out the general's decision to the army and to execute it.

On 7 August, the daily order spelled out in detail the quantity and type of material needed for the new infantry uniforms. All of it was to be made of cotton.

Line Infantry: dark blue coat with red collar and cuffs, lined white (so turnbacks are white), wood buttons. White gaiter-trousers.

Light Infantry: all dark blue coat and gaiter-trousers.

Presumably, grenadiers and carabiniers retained their scarlet wool epaulettes.

On 19 September, the first uniforms were issued to the troops as per the daily order:

|  | Coats | Overcoats | Trousers |
|---|---|---|---|
| 2nd Light Demi-Brigade | 400 | 1,000 | 400 |
| 4th Light Demi-Brigade | 500 | 1,100 | 500 |
| 21st Light Demi-Brigade | 800 | 1,700 | 800 |
| 22nd Light Demi-Brigade | 400 | 1,000 | 400 |
| 9th Line Demi-Brigade | 600 | 1,300 | 600 |
| 13th Line Demi-Brigade | 600 | 1,600 | 600 |
| 18th Line Demi-Brigade | 700 | 1,500 | 700 |
| 19th Line Demi-Brigade Grenadiers | 300 | 500 | 300 |
| 25th Line Demi-Brigade | 500 | 1,300 | 500 |
| 32nd Line Demi-Brigade | 700 | 1,600 | 700 |
| 61st Line Demi-Brigade | 600 | 1,400 | 600 |
| 69th Line Demi-Brigade | 1,200 | 1,200 | 0 |
| 75th Line Demi-Brigade | 800 | 1,700 | 800 |
| 85th Line Demi-Brigade | 700 | 1,500 | 700 |
| 88th Line Demi-Brigade | 500 | 1,100 | 500 |

In the meantime it had been decided also to manufacture and issue overcoats so as to provide protection against the cold night time. Although we do not have the specifics of these coats at this point in time we can assume they are similar to the ones which were issued later on and which were of white or light coloured wool with in some cases light blue collar and cuffs. As can be seen from the numbers, overcoats were the priority given that the autumn and then winter period were becoming quite cold.

If we have Bernoyer's limited description and the materials detail from the order, we have otherwise very little iconographic information on this first version of the specific Egyptian uniform for the army. The best known source is the oil draft sketch made for a painting showing the Battle of Nazareth in Syria by Baron Gros. Indeed, by the end of 1798, the army had been clothed with the new uniforms and therefore marched into Syria with it. Upon his return to France, Bonaparte commissioned Gros to execute a painting illustrating the battle of Nazareth. We know that Gros received items of clothing and equipment but also information from participants. This has been the basis for all the reconstructions done by 20th century artists. What we see is a coatee very much like the Austrian or later British type. The trousers are more difficult to figure out but one soldier loading his musket is visible down to his feet and we can make out the fact that there is what seems to be a 'separation' below the knee at ankle level. Obviously the 'gaiters' were a slight tightening of the pants making them look very much like tightened

Bonaparte at the Battle of the Pyramids, coloured engraving after Baron Gros' painting. The original painting by Gros was done a few years after the events but is still contemporary to a large degree. As all paintings then commissioned it is a propaganda piece and certainly does not represent with absolute accuracy the situation on that day. Murat, bare-headed, is at the front, whereas he was then under the command of Dumas who led the cavalry. To this day, it is one of the most famous images of the Egyptian expedition.

(1)

The Army of the Orient leaves for Egypt. At the end of the 19th century, in celebration of the French Revolution and 1st Empire centennial, several picture books were published. This image is taken from one of these, *Victoires et Conquêtes des Armées Françaises*. It made extensive use of period prints or paintings, adding colour to them when necessary. This specific image has its origin in an uncoloured Martinet print published barely a few years after the expedition.

The Battle of the Pyramids. From a print by Martinet. Vernet and Martinet published prints a few years after the battle. Baron Lejeune painted one of his most famous pieces, however he was not present but based it like the printmakers on eyewitness accounts.

The Battle of the Nile. Coloured print by Weber. The explosion of the *Orient* was the centre piece of the battle for all artists. This excellent print is no exception but also shows the ferocious hand-to-hand fighting which occurred all across the sea.

The Revolt in Cairo. After a painting by Girodet. Girodet's original work is a massive and spectacular painting which can be considered one of the first romantic and orientalist paintings. It depicts the brutality of the fighting but also stresses the beauty of the uniforms and even more the richness of the oriental garments. Like many Napoleonic period paintings, it was done as a propaganda piece.

The fight at Nazareth. Taken from a rare period print by Caraffe, it was probably produced in the very first years of the consulate as the look of the dragoons seems fairly accurate and the same can be said of the Syrians.

Bonaparte and the sick at Jaffa. After a painting by Baron Gros. Another very well-known propaganda piece. It was commissioned to counter all the negative stories conveyed by the British press.

The Battle of Aboukir. After another well-known painting by Baron Lejeune. again, Lejeune was not present but he was well informed by others who were there.

The French army in Syene (upper-Egypt). After a painting by Tardieu, done during the Consulate. The uniforms are of course those worn when the painting was painted and not those worn in Egypt. There are very few images of Desaix' campaigns. We do have drawings done on the spot by Vivant Denon, but, the fighting being mainly hit-and-run affairs, it did not inspire much. Here again this is a propaganda piece showing the military discovering the ancient relics of Egypt.

The French in Cairo. This rather comic image by JOB is taken from the book, l'Épopée du Costume Militaire, which is a history of French military costume aimed at a large audience. This is one of the very first attempts at illustrating the multi-coloured dress worn in Egypt. But what actually is truly interesting is the depiction here of those 'donkey races' in the streets of Cairo which French soldiers seemed to have been fond of, much to the dismay of the locals!

French Revolutionary-era line infantry: This splendid watercolour by military artist Lucien Rousselot is actually part of a series showing the evolution of the French infantry from 1645 to 1815. On the left a fusilier wears the regulation dress as set out as of 1792-1793. It follows the 1786 regulation slightly modified in 1791, but the coat colour is now blue (instead of white) and regimental distinctions have given way to white (for lapels and turnbacks) and red (for collar and cuffs). On the right an NCO, identified as such by his sabre, is in more of a campaign mode. The breeches and gaiters have been replaced by trousers made of locally sourced cloth (perhaps mattress ticking). His sabre is a 1776 pattern which would last well into the Empire.

Around 1797, Grasset de Saint-Sauveur published a series of colour plates showing French administrative as well as military uniforms. These, produced at about the time of the expedition beautifully show what the general officers and their staff looked like.

Above left: A commander in chief, typically a général de division but with a tricolour centre plume on his hat and a bicolour sash (more than often replaced by a tricolour one).

Above right: Général de Division – red sash.

Left: Général de Brigade – blue sash.

Above left: Aides; left general adjutant; right an ADC to a général de division (red arm band) with a sky blue collar.

Above right: General adjutant with the typical bar lace on collar and cuffs. He wears the typical general officer's coat. Actually in the depths of the French archives, the author found a caricature of a staff officer on night patrol during the final siege of Cairo by the British, wearing exactly such a coat.

Right: Commissary. This is the official uniform Daure or Sucy would have worn. However it is more than likely that on a daily basis, the tricolour neck-ribbon would not have been used.

The 1798-1799 infantry uniform worn in Egypt as depicted in this large watercolour by Boisselier. In this case this is the 9th Line Demi-Brigade (red tuft). Boisselier has closely followed Baron Gerard's painting of the Battle of Nazareth.

This stunning watercolour by Boisselier shows a fusilier of the 9th Line Demi-Brigade according to the 'Kléber uniform'. Boisselier has also chosen to show a cap which is inspired by the Chasseriau document. The 9th is one of the best documented units as Pepin's orderly book was available to Vanson and parts of it were published by him.

Egypt cap and the various infantry tufts. The author has used a single type of cap to show the variations according to the daily order dated 13 September 1798. However, it is highly probable that multiple variations of cap designs existed.

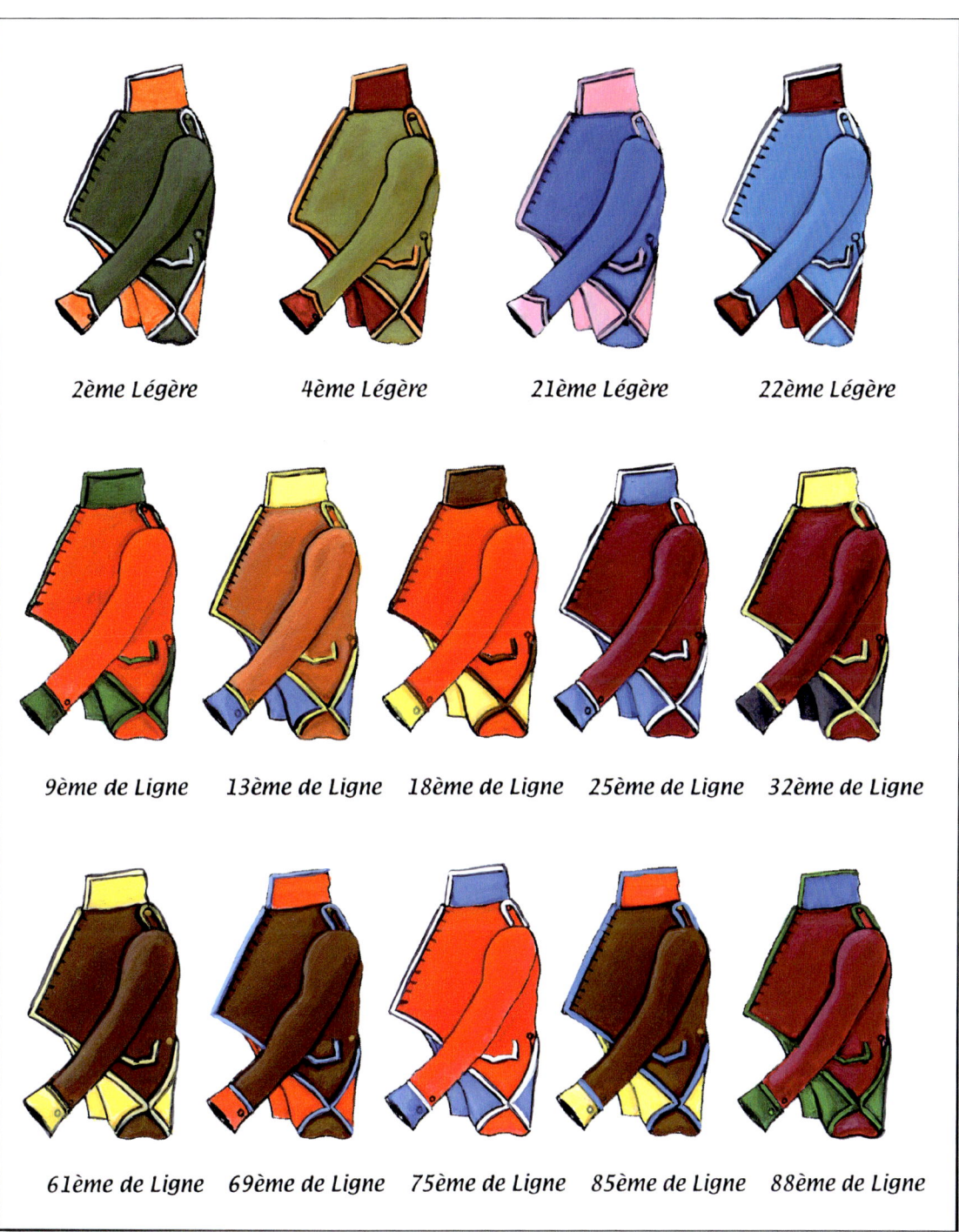

Infantry coats Late 1799-1801. Based on the actual cloth samples found in the French archives, the author has reconstructed what each demi-brigade was wearing. The colouring matches as best as possible the actual cloth samples.

The 'Chasseriau Documents'. The 25th, 69th, 85th and 88th Line Demi-Brigades. All but that showing the 88th are actual original watercolours form the period. The 88th is a facsimile copy which was done by Lucien Rousselot for Jean Brunon (probably in the 1930s).

25th Line Demi-Brigade. The drummer wears a simple coat with swallows' nests which seem to have been systematic in French infantry at that period. Note that the sapper and the grenadier wear a bearskin.

69th Line Demi-Brigade. Note the bastion shaped light blue lace at the collar. The author has not yet chased down later iconography for the 69th line, but it is quite possible that the unit continued wearing such lace. Note that the grenadier wears a hat, not a cap

85th Line Demi-Brigade. This is by far the most amazing plate. First the drummer who wears a light orange dolman with lace, faced red with red lace and sky blue piping. In many ways, this is in line with the original Bonaparte order to have drummers and trumpeters wear dolmans. Then the grenadier has a bearskin with frontal plate. Again, like the depiction of the 25th, this implies grenadiers managed to keep bearskins and probably find a way to replace them. Finally the fusilier does not wear a cap, but a hat. Again, this should not come as full surprise as the cap was hated by many as being ugly.

88th Line Demi-Brigade. The copy by Rousselot. Although this depiction is well known, now alongside the other three it takes a whole new meaning. Visibly none of the grenadier companies wore the cap. Lace decorations at the collar existed probably out of the wish of the chef de brigade to distinguish his men. Finally, drummers wore swallows' nests but dolmans also existed. We can only wish that other such documents surface one day to complete our view of the Army of the Orient.

Studies in watercolour by Boisselier of the 'Kléber Uniform'. These are all based on the one document then known (Chasseriau) and various drawings of the cap. The last figure is a grenadier of the 13th line in white greatcoat at the battle of Alexandria. As their coats were a reddish brown, they could be confused with the enemy and were asked to wear their greatcoats.

These drawings were initially copied from a major work of coloured plates by Boisselier on the Army of the Orient. The current whereabouts of the work in itself is unknown, but black and white tracings were done in the 1950s or 1960s. The author has used these to colour them according to the most recent information found on the actual colours worn by those units.

Fusilier, 13th Line Demi-Brigade.   Fusilier, 18th Line Demi-Brigade.

Fusilier, 25th Line Demi-Brigade.

Chasseur, 2nd Light Demi-Brigade.

Carabinier, 21st Light Demi-Brigade.

Chasseur, 22nd Light Demi-Brigade; note that Boisselier has actually shown an African 'recruit' for this unit.

The Nautical Legion. These two figures by Boisselier are based on the descriptions given by Lienhart & Humbert at the end of the 19th century. We do not have any period representation of the Nautical Legion.

Native Guides by Benigni. Whether the native guides actually existed as a formal unit or not, we do know that local native units were raised. They all probably looked very much like this. Benigni, oddly enough, forgot to make visible the French tricolour cockade which was to be worn by all troops and most certainly local ones.

The 'Chasseriau Document' dragoons (top-left, 3rd; top-right 14th; bottom-left 15th; bottom-right, 18th) are all fairly similar, but do show differences. The 3rd and 14th have black helmets which are probably made of leather. All wear the typical cavalry overalls which were popular all throughout the period. The 15th actually wears the regulation dragoon boots and breeches, whereas the norm in Egypt should have been hussar boots.

14th Dragoons NCO; Boisselier black and white tracing set to colour by the author.

3rd Dragoons trumpeter. The 3rd Dragoons was the only dragoon regiment to have its trumpeters wearing red, the other dragoon regiments had them wear light orange. A Boisselier watercolour.

(24)

There are almost no contemporary illustrations of the 7th *bis* Hussars. There is the Battle of Aboukir painting in the Tarbes hussar museum, and there are also possibly some troopers of the regiment in Italy depicted in a painting currently in Versailles. Finally there is this 'reconstruction'. We know for fact that before 1871, the Tuileries palace library housed several volumes of uniform plates done by Hoffmann. These were burnt during the Paris commune, but descriptions of them survived. In the 1900s, a reconstruction of the volume devoted to Revolutionary period hussar regiments was done. This is therefore the plate from that reproduction showing the 7th *bis*.

A striking watercolour by Boissleier done in 1917 and largely based on Eugene Lami's illustration of the Coptic Legion.

Parade dress around 1800 using Dromedary François' memoirs as well as a document in Larrey's collection.

Dromedaries have been a favourite with French military artist for some time. There are several reasons to this. First we do have more documentation on them than on any other single unit. Cavalier's personal papers have all been in the archives for some time and have been amply looked at. Also, we do have various quasi-contemporary iconographies (including a plate by Goddard and Booth probably done using eyewitness accounts from British troops). Over the next pages we see three more original watercolour plates by Boisselier.

A dromedary officer around 1800. This is a copy of the watercolour done by Valmont which is in one of his volumes at the Bibliotheque Nationale de France. Valmont, a naval officer, amassed a considerable amount of first-hand documentation and painted his plates between 1820 and 1870.

A Dromedary on campaign. This is directly taken using Cavalier's orderly book in the archives.

A dromedary gunner NCO around 1800. The dromedaries were assigned some artillery pieces but in effect the uniform of the gunners were in no way different from those of the other troopers. This is again taken from Cavalier's orderly book.

Dromedary on campaign; watercolour by Eugene Leliepvre. This is again taken from the orderly book and shows the dromedary wearing loose oriental trousers.

Dromedary and dromedary trumpeter on campaign watercolour by Eugene Leliepvre. Again the orderly book is the source, but not the only one. The only item of original dress to have come down to us is a full uniform of trumpeter for the Dromedaries. This remarkable piece is in the French Army Museum where it can be seen and examined. The cloth is fairly rough, as is the lace, but it is quite striking at a distance being all red with white lace. Here the cavalry campaign overalls are worn rather than tight hussar-style breeches.

## UNIFORMS – 'THE MOST BEAUTIFUL SIGHT THE EYE COULD BEHOLD'

French line infantry (left) and Line infantry officer (right) by Hauck. These wonderful prints by Hauck were done in Holland around 1795-1796. They very accurately show how French revolutionary infantry looked on campaign. At the start of the expedition, the infantry would have looked very much like this.

breeches sub-knee level. Rousselot in his own version exaggerated this to the point of making them similar to the golfing trousers very much in fashion in the 1920s-1930s, something much more reflective of his own period than what was probably adopted. It is no surprise that such a coat was chosen as the French had been indeed much exposed to the Austrian uniform which had been designed for economy and suited well the warm Italian climate. Cotton was, of course, in ample supply in Egypt and it proved fairly easy to get enough in blue to dress up the infantry.

As one will have certainly noted, Bernoyer's letter does not mention either head dress for the infantry or uniforms for other service branches. Yet, decisions were also taken in both matters.

The infantry hat had been, and would continue to be, a source of discontent with both troops and officers. We know through iconographic evidence it would be used to drink water from, and again perspiration and just campaigning would transform it into a rather unpleasant looking thing. Furthermore, it hardly provided protection from violent sunlight or the fierce Mameluke sabres. It is through the mention of coloured tufts in the 14 September daily order and of grenades to be applied to the new 'casques' (helmets) adopted for infantry in the 18 September daily order that we learn of the new head-dress. This new item has proven ever since to be the most elusive and mysterious piece of uniform worn by the French army. Again, very little iconographic evidence has survived, and, yet again, only Baron Gros' painting can be assumed to represent what was worn in 1798-1799.

The first intriguing aspect is quite simply the French words used to describe it. The very first mention uses the word 'casque' which is literally helmet and is typically used to describe a rigid head-dress like the 1791 Tarleton style helmet. Later on, the word 'casquette' is used which can be translated as cap and literally means 'small helmet'. We do have for the later period under Kléber more iconography as we shall see, and indeed it does look like a tufted cap. What we however see in Gros' painting looks much more like a rather rigid leather helmet with a fairly large crest or tuft.

Have any of these caps survived? There are possibly two. The first one has been seen by the author in a private collection and seems to be based on the 1791 model which has been modified to have its fake leopard-skin flap shortened, attached with laces in the front, so it can be untied and brought down to shield the neck and ears from the sun. It clearly shows that it did not hold the large 1791 crest, but only a reduced one, basically a tuft. Another one is said to have been present in another private collection and was reproduced by Jacques Domange in one of his plates devoted to the army in Egypt. This cap had grenades on it and Domange also showed some caps with the light infantry motif of horns.

In any case the caps had therefore on top a wool tuft which helped identify the unit

2nd Light Demi-Brigade: green
4th Light Demi-Brigade: green and white
21st Light Demi-Brigade: green and yellow
22nd Light Demi-Brigade: green and red
9th Line Demi-Brigade: red
13th Line Demi-Brigade: blue
18th Line Demi-Brigade: black
19th Line Demi-Brigade: yellow
25th Line Demi-Brigade: red and white
32nd Line Demi-Brigade: blue and white
61st Line Demi-Brigade: black and white
69th Line Demi-Brigade: yellow and white
75th Line Demi-Brigade: blue and red
85th Line Demi-Brigade: yellow and red
88th Line Demi-Brigade: yellow and blue
Foot Guides: tricolour

As can be seen, there was quite some logic. Light infantry had a combination involving green, the typical colour of light troops, while line infantry avoided that colour while using other simple basic colours. Guides, as part of staff, displayed red, white, and blue. How were those colours set up on the tufts? Again, there is no conclusive evidence. Most artists have shown them one above the other, but in some cases one horizontally next to the other. Let us not forget Herbert Knötel, who also showed the colours displayed in alternate stripes, which is also a possibility but Knötel showed this only for the later period under Kléber.

The other question which arises is whether the cap was generally adopted or not. Again, evidence shows that this was not always the case. Grenadiers and carabiniers seem to have resisted this. In a naïve watercolour representing himself lying in hospital wounded, Carabinier Vaxelaire of the 2nd Light Demi-Brigade shows a hat with a small carrot plume. Other iconography continues to show hats being worn, especially with dropping red plumes for the elite companies. Indeed having had one in hand, the author can readily state that the helmet was a fairly ugly piece of dress and one can understand the men wishing to keep as much as possible their hats.

As stated in the order dated 18 September, grenadier and carabinier caps were to have two grenades, presumably one on each side and probably of metal.

The same order introduced yet another major change – all trumpeters and drummers of the army were to wear a sky blue dolman using the '400 that are currently in storage'. This was indeed the type of dress and colour used already by the Guides trumpeters. To have this extended to all other units can only be explained by the need make bets use of these dolmans. Was this formally enforced? We honestly do not know. We are certain however, as will be shown, that other colours were adopted and/or worn by cavalry units in 1799. Likewise, although the use of dolmans for infantry drummers, fifers, and musicians is proven and we have now graphic evidence of this under Kléber and Menou, the colours that were used varied.

In the other decisions taken in the early autumn of 1798, infantrymen were ordered to carry a metal flask for water and all ranks that did not carry a long arm up to now (such as officers and drummers.) were to carry one, albeit a short one such as a rifled musket or a cavalry musketoon. Both these orders resulted from the early campaigning.

The need for having water carried around is obvious. The light metal flask was actually an optional regulation item that soldiers could buy. All probably had by themselves equipped with some form of gourd. The metal flask however would rust and leave a rather bad aftertaste in the water. It never proved popular.

Muskets were very quickly carried systematically. Indeed, increasing the overall firepower of a unit and ensuring one would be able to defend oneself without engaging in close quarter combat proved a necessity.

We have no formal trace of similar orders for artillery and engineers. However, correspondence from Sucy's successor Daure implies that the same changes were adopted. The cap, however seems to have been even less popular and most iconographic evidence shows hats being worn.

What of the cavalry? They were much less impacted than infantry. A lighter waistcoat and overalls (called 'pantalons d'écurie') were adopted. Officers were ordered to carry short shoulder arms. Many actually had equipped themselves with Mameluke blunderbusses. Arab-style capes with hoods also became popular with dragoons, as well as locally-sourced Egyptian saddles. Again, officers across all units had made much of the loot they had gathered after the Pyramids and when entering Cairo. Over time, dragoons adopted hussar-style boots which were far more comfortable and made much more sense given the style of campaigning they had to face.

# THE FRENCH ARMY OF THE ORIENT 1798–1801

French light infantry by Seele. This contemporary coloured print done by Seele in Germany around 1795-1797 shows the ragged look of the French light infantry on campaign. The distinctive short coat and overall dark blue appearance is quite noticeable. The light infantrymen at the beginning of the campaign in Egypt probably looked very much like the centre figure with a hat (a carabinier, given his plume and epaulettes).

As indicated earlier, a new regulation had been introduced for general officers and staff on 8 August 1798. This was most probably implemented over the late autumn of 1798 and early 1799. The portraits we have by Dutertre typically show undress uniforms with little to no lace for senior officers.

We do have written evidence that a specific general's helmet was introduced. On 25 January 1799, Daure wrote to his chief clothing administrator: 'Citizen, the general-in-chief asks for eight leather helmets with rich gold embroidery and flowing plumes. You will have this readied with no delay'. Furthermore, in Desgenettes' notes, he specifically remembers that Bonaparte showed up once with a roman style helmet with plumes which made him look ridiculous. Finally, at Kléber's funeral, several testimonials state that 'the general's helmet was laid on top of his coffin'. So, we can be fairly sure that an enriched version of the infantry cap/helmet was designed for parade use for generals, probably only those managing divisions and present in Cairo.

As mentioned, with Sucy having left for France he was replaced by the young and extremely gifted administrator Daure. We are lucky in that all of Daure's archives have been given to the French army archives. As of the date of 22 November 1798 up to his dismissal by Menou in 1800, we have all of Daure's correspondence dealing with his clothing administration. Indeed the very first letter on that day is to ask Thorin, chief clothing administrator, to speed up the production of overcoats as 'nights are becoming very chilly' and that the very first of these coats need to be delivered to the infantry demi-brigades which are 'constantly on the march'.

Five days later, Daure asked Thorin to look into the quality of the cotton cloth used, as several units were complaining of its poor quality. These issues were probably either solved or set aside, as the troops continued to be outfitted and, as we saw, marched into Syria wearing the cotton uniforms. One small change however had been made, to ensure the gaiters would hold properly and no sand or grit would get in, a strap had been fixed which went under the sole. These straps did not last long and thus proved inefficient and were abandoned.

## The Kléber Uniforms

As the army came back from Syria in the late spring of 1799, conclusions could be drawn on the cotton uniforms. They were most certainly a major improvement over the heavy European uniforms, but the cotton cloth had proven far too fragile, and, yet again, the army had to be completely re-uniformed. The cut of the coat was visibly satisfactory, and, despite their ugliness the caps had proven adequate. The obvious solution was to go back to woollen cloth, although of lighter weight, while keeping the new design.

However, if cotton was plentiful in Egypt, getting hold of enough blue-coloured woollen cloth proved impossible. The actual supply mainly came from a firm ran by a Genoese family, the Pini Brothers, who had establishments in Genoa but also Marseilles and Alexandria. Daure and his services worked with them to source whatever woollen cloth was available in sufficient quantity to clothe the army.

The Aboukir campaign obviously delayed the process and it was only on 24 August 1798 that a new daily order was issued by Bonaparte indicating what the uniforms for the army for Year VIII would be. Blue wool was to be reserved for artillery and engineers, and green for cavalry, whilst the infantry would be dressed in various combinations of colour involving red, black, grey, and puce (that is to say, 'flea' or dark brown). The coatee for the infantry continued to be the design used for the cotton uniforms. A light waistcoat was to be issued also. There would be off-white trousers made of 'strong cloth' (probably serge) for line infantry, while light infantry, artillery, and engineers would have dark blue trousers of the same make. Horse artillery, dragoons, hussars, and chasseurs continued to wear their uniforms and all cavalry to wear hussar boots. Each infantryman to receive one cap (and the word used is 'casquette', i.e. cap).

As we know, Bonaparte left Egypt soon afterwards, and Kléber was left to deal with this issue. It is only on 1 October 1799 that a daily order stipulated which colours were to be worn for each unit. However, when came the time to execute this order, two factors came into play. The first is that Kléber and some of the unit officers changed in some cases their mind in terms of colours to be used for a given unit. More importantly, the actual colour shades and volumes per colour that landed from the Pini Brothers into the army stores varied from the initial plan. This forced further changes which could have a knock-on impact on the actual execution.

General Vanson, who was the first to do an exhaustive study of the uniforms of the army in Egypt in the mid-1890s, went through Daure's correspondence to come up with a corrected table for the uniforms worn. Yet, when Vanson wrote his article he had no iconography to back up his findings, only the Gros painting which showed the previous uniform. It was only after the First World War, in the early 1920s, that two documents surfaced relative to these uniforms.

A period watercolour showing a drummer, sapper, grenadier and fusilier of the 88th Line Demi-Brigade. The agreed-upon colours that were issued stated:

coat: crimson
turnbacks: green
cuffs: green
cuff piping: white
collar: green
collar piping: white

# THE FRENCH ARMY OF THE ORIENT 1798–1801

Another drawing by Boisselier showing the great-coat and famous 'pike' as worn and used by the infantry in 1798 and early 1799 (and, in the case of the pike, quickly discarded).

The watercolour was then owned by the Baron Chasseriau, famous art collector and president of 'La Sabretache' and son of a famous 19th century architect who had built several buildings, including the French consulate, in Alexandria in the 1830s. It is probably there or in relation to his stay in Egypt that this document had come in his possession. All the types shown in it matched perfectly (including the yellow and blue tuft) with one important difference. The coat was a light purple rather than the expected deep purplish red known as crimson (cramoisi). It did however show the (in)famous cap, which looked more like a jockey cap built from several strips of leather. It also proved that grenadiers had indeed continued to wear the hat and sappers the bearskin.

Less than a year later, another drawing surfaced in Alsace having come from Dr Bockenheim former surgeon the Mamelukes and Imperial Guard Chasseurs, but more importantly former surgeon of the Dromedaries. It showed an infantryman in very much the same outfit with a very slightly different cap.

It is based on both of these images, and the work done by Vanson, that Rousselot, Boisselier, Rigo, and all other artists based their works all throughout the rest of the 20th century. Then, at the very end of the 1990s, the author of this work was going through various archive boxes of the Army of Orient in the French war archives when he stumbled upon a fascinating two page document. Entitled 'Uniform of the Troops of the Army of Orient', it simply had descriptions of the colours worn by each unit, and, more importantly, actual cloth samples next to each line. While very few of them were missing, it also indicated a few differences in terms of actual colours for some units versus the Vanson study. More importantly, for a colour with the same name, the samples could vary in shade. For example, the 'crimson' used for the 13th Line Demi Brigade was a dark red, while that for the 88th turned out to be reddish purple – thus matching perfectly with the Chasseriau document. The green of the 4th Light Demi-Brigade, previously assumed to be a light green, was in fact a brownish olive-green!

But the most important find was still to come. At the end of 2016, a total of seven 'military' watercolours showed up for sale at a Paris auction. To the author's surprise, three were similar to the Chasseriau document but showing the 25th, 69th and 85th Line Demi-Brigades, while the other four showed the 3rd, 14th, 15th and 18th Dragoons. As one might by then have expected, the colours shown matched perfectly the samples stored in the archives.

It is possible that, either the very final implementation for some units again diverged due to lack of cloth, or that for Year IX, units had to be dressed again and changes made. The former is more probable than the latter. In any case we now have four period images showing what the infantry units looked like and we can safely assume the colour samples presented in the document in the archives represent what was actually worn by the Army of the Orient as of late 1799 and used at the Battle of Heliopolis and later during the British invasion.

Yet again, these 'new' images confirm that grenadiers did not wear the cap but had stuck to the hat or even kept their bearskin (including a brass plate with a grenade for the 85th Line Demi-Brigade). For all but the 85th, drummers wear the same coat as the other troops but with swallow's nests as epaulettes. The 85th drummer is fascinating in that he wears a dolman, not light blue but light orange with red lace, cuffs, collar and swallow's nest: basically displaying the colours of the tuft of the 85th. This matches another testimonial from Grandjean who was yet another senior clothing administrator and who had indicated that units had dressed their drummers and musicians in all kinds of colours, those in crimson dressing them in light blue, some in black and some 'adorned with lace'.

It is probable that these watercolours were part of a series which showed all of the units. Will we ever see them all surface again? We are already quite lucky to now have such wealth of primary sources on a topic which had been so hotly debated amongst specialists for over a century.

Army of Orient infantry coats – source: detailed table with cloth samples in French war archives (Service Historique de la Défense)

| Demi-Brigade | Coat | Turnbacks | Cuffs | Cuff Piping | Collar | Collar Piping |
|---|---|---|---|---|---|---|
| 2nd Light | Dark Green | Light orange | Light orange | White | Light orange | White |
| 4th Light | Olive Green | Red | Red | Light Orange | Red | Light Orange |
| 21st Light | Sky blue | Pink | Pink | Pink | Pink | Pink |
| 22nd Light | Sky blue | Crimson | Crimson | White | Crimson | White |
| 9th Line | Scarlet | Green | Green | Green | Green | Red |
| 13th Line | Crimson | Sky blue | Sky blue | Yellow | Yellow | Yellow |
| 18th Line | Scarlet | Yellow | Yellow | Brown | Brown | Brown |
| 25th Line | Crimson | Sky blue | Sky Blue | White | Sky blue | White |
| 32nd Line | Crimson | Black | Black | Yellow | Yellow | Yellow |
| 61st Line | Brown | Yellow | Yellow | Yellow | Yellow | Yellow |
| 69th Line | Brown | Scarlet | Scarlet | Blue | Scarlet | Blue |
| 75th Line | Scarlet | Blue | Blue | White | Blue | White |
| 85th Line | Brown | Yellow | Yellow | Blue | Scarlet | Blue |
| 88th Line | Crimson | Green | Green | Green | Sky blue | Green |

It is also to be noted that although these colours applied to all ranks, officers were to wear a different coat. Kléber specifically mentioned this and indicated that officers were expected to have a 'long coat'. Put simply, a similar coat to the solders' but with long tails. Indeed this is confirmed by excerpts from Chef de Brigade Pepin of the 9th Line Demi-Brigade's orderly book, quoted by Vanson. Pepin had a coat model made for his officers, shown to them and approved. Incidentally, in the same text it is mentioned that musicians and drummers were to wear inverted colours, which for the 9th meant a green coat with red distinctions. This was later to be kept as a tradition in the future 9th Line Infantry throughout the Consular and Imperial periods.

As for the cap, aside from the depiction we have in the watercolours, we have another document from the late Roger Forthoffer's archives. Forthoffer was a major French uniformologist from the 1940s until his death in the early 1980s. One of his ancestors had been in Egypt and seems to have brought back a number of drawings including an interesting page showing three cap models, supposedly coming from Kléber's own archives. The first model is very similar to the one known and shows a unit number on the front possibly with grenades on each side. The second is a reinforced model with metal strips and a front plate with unit number and a grenade. The third is the most interesting as it is a model for officers with a metal crest similar to that of cavalry helmets supporting a coloured hair crest. Whether these models were implemented or not, we have no other evidence, but given how many exotic variations were adopted, we cannot rule these out.

Other dismounted units followed the same rules as the infantry and adopted a woollen uniform.

Army of Orient coats – source: detailed table with cloth samples in French war archives (Service Historique de la Défense)

| Unit | Coat | Turnbacks | Cuffs | Cuff Piping | Collar | Collar Piping |
|---|---|---|---|---|---|---|
| Foot Artillery | Dark blue | Red | Red | Red | Red | Red |
| Artillery workers | Dark blue | Cream | Cream | Cream) | Dark blue | Cream |
| Sappers | Dark blue | Dark blue | Dark blue | Purplish-Red | Purplish-Red | Purplish-Red |
| Miners | Dark blue | Dark blue | Black | Red | Black | Red |
| Balloon corps | Dark blue | Green | Green | White | Green | White |
| Engineering workers | Dark blue | Dark Blue | Red | Red | Red | Red |
| Artillery train | Brownish-Yellow | Brown | Brown | Cream | Brown | Cream |
| School | Light Brown | Brown | Brown | White | Brown | White |

The artillery train, initially a civilian corps, had been militarised and was given a coat colour called in French 'carmelite', meaning colour of the dress worn by Carmel nuns, that is to say a tan or brownish yellow. In a similar manner, students of the 'French School' (i.e. mathematics school) who could be civilians or former military personal, were also given a brownish coat.

All used as headdress the cap or hat. We do not have formal indications of the tuft colour, but we should assume that artillery and related services had a red tuft, and engineering services a black one. As for the train, probably a red one, while it is known that the school, being assimilated to staff, had a tricolour one.

What of the regular French cavalry and guides?

## UNIFORMS – 'THE MOST BEAUTIFUL SIGHT THE EYE COULD BEHOLD'

French Revolutionary-era light artillery by Seele. Again from the 1795-1797 period. It shows the cavalry-style uniforms worn by French light artillery.

Guides do not seem to have been impacted by the above decisions – even for the Foot Guides, we have no mention of coatees being made for them. We should then assume they kept their initial dress but with a cap. The same goes for the Mounted Guides, although as mentioned above, quite a few pieces of Mameluke equipment were adopted.

The cavalry is specifically indicated as keeping its former uniforms – however a few changes were made.

As stated, hussar boots became the norm across all units, however the contemporary watercolour showing the 15th Dragoons still shows regular boots. Light waistcoats were adopted, as were corduroy breeches for dragoons. Cavalry overalls became quasi-universal wear and are indeed shown on three of the four contemporary watercolours. The regulation brass dragoon helmet seems to have been replaced in some instances by a similar model but with a leather body as shown for the 3rd and 14th Dragoons in these paintings.

Hussars and chasseurs do not seem to have made massive changes. The mirliton shako gave way to one somewhat similar to the future Napoleonic shako but with a flame. When did this happen? The key sources for this are two paintings in the hussar museum in Tarbes. One shows General Verdier's wife wearing feminised version of a 7th *bis* Hussar uniform which includes such a shako. The other one shows the Battle of Aboukir with men of the 7th *bis* Hussars and 22nd Chasseurs types again with similar shakos.

As for trumpeters, the sky blue dolman does not seem to have survived too long. According to an order from Daure dated 3 November 1799, the 3rd Dragoons' trumpeters were to wear scarlet and all other dragoon trumpeters, 'aurore' (light orange). For hussar trumpeters, the scarlet uniform seems to have held on, and the light orange one with green breeches for chasseurs.

Finally, as a general rule, not long after Menou became commander-in-chief, the order was given to have units adopt what were called 'Arab overcoats', most probably long wool coats with hoods to provide adequate protection against the cold or sandstorms.

Aside from these regulation French troops, the units which were created locally were also provided for with uniforms which evolved slightly over time.

## Dromedaries

The Dromedaries were by far the most exotic unit created and were also to shine as a unit, especially on parade. After Bernoyer's initial attempt at a 'localised' uniform in the autumn of 1798 for Bonaparte's very first project for camel-mounted couriers, the dromedary unit was set up in early 1799 with a distinctive oriental look.

The overall flavour for both parade and campaign dress was to be very hussar style. On parade, a long oriental style red coat with white hussar braiding was worn over a sky blue dolman and Hungarian breeches. A white turban was initially worn, but gave way to a red 'cahook', or oriental shako, with tricolour plumes. For day-to-day dress, Dromedaries wore a sky blue dolman with white lace, sky blue or red hussar breeches. As headdress, a hat with a red or black tipped red plume. On campaign, Dromedaries could wear all kinds of combinations of dress: retain the sky blue dolman, wear a sky blue stable coat, have cavalry overalls, or wear baggy oriental trousers in either red or white. Initially armed also with a long pike, they retained it until the autumn of 1799, as a letter to Kléber from the regimental commander, Cavalier, asks for these weapons to be officially abandoned as they had proven to be of little or no use. In fact, all Dromedaries were former infantrymen and, as such, they were far more effective with a dragoon musket. Another interesting letter to Kléber, signed by all the regimental officers, indicates that the cost of their uniforms far exceeded what they had expected and that of other units.

## Nautical Legion

Organised after the naval disaster at Aboukir Bay in the late summer of 1798, the Nautical Legion regrouped all navy personnel who no longer had ships. To expedite its clothing, it was decided to put to good use all the red cloth that had been seized in Malta where it was used for the Order of Malta troops. This resulted in the Legion having a distinctive red uniform of the same cut as the new infantry coatee. Cuffs were sky blue as was all piping, however sources vary as to the colour of the collar (white, red, or sky blue) and for turnbacks (sky blue or white). All these variations probably co-existed depending on the amount of cloth available. As a headdress, the seamen kept their typical leather top hat with red round tuft and cockades. Officers wore coats of a similar colour as the men but either with long tails or of a regular 1786 cut.

What of the second Nautical Legion created in the spring of 1799? Unlike the first one it was formed by pulling together all navy personnel.

We actually have no concrete evidence of any specific uniform having been issued and it is quite possible that men kept the dress they had before being incorporated. Traditionally French military artists have assumed that the former Nautical Legion dress was once again used, but again, there is no written or iconographic evidence of this.

## Maltese Legion

The uniform given to the Maltese Legion was quite distinct from the one that Maltese troops used to wear prior to the French seizure of the island. It was green faced red. According to the few sources we have, especially Valmont's watercolours done probably in the 1830s-1840s, the coat was of regular 1786 pattern with cuffs, collar, lapels and turnbacks all in red piped white. The headdress was an infantry hat with a red carrot tuft. Red grenadiers' epaulettes were also worn for the grenadiers. White trousers were worn; Valmont shows them as very baggy. The Legion received the new coatee in green with red collar, turnbacks, and cuffs in December 1799 along with a tufted cap for the fusiliers, the tuft being yellow.

## Coptic Legion

We do have more evidence for the Coptic Legion than for the Maltese. The earliest depiction is in the Vernet-Lami series which was done in the late 1810s. The Legion wore a green coatee with collar, turnbacks, and cuffs faced yellow. Grenadiers had red epaulettes and probably wore a hat with a hanging plume. They seem to have worn tight fitting breeches of a yellow-brown colour. Caps have been assumed for fusiliers to have had a yellow tuft, but no formal evidence exists.

## Greek Legion

Again, Vernet-Lami showed a depiction of the Greek Legion in their series, and this was again showed by Valmont in his watercolours. There seems to have been no real uniform but men wore their national costume with baggy trousers, a short vest, and a red fez with a blue tail. A tricolour cockade was probably displayed somewhere on the uniform.

## Other Native Units

All other native units: Syrian Janissaries, Syrian Legion, Mamelukes, and so forth. wore their own native dress. As the Syrian Legion was being organised, Daure mentioned clearly to Kléber that they should retain their native Syrian dress distinctive from that of the local Egyptians. In all of these cases, a tricolour cockade would be worn. Indeed in one of the early Janissary formations, very simple tricolour flags were given to these units. All of the armament, equipment, etc. came from surplus, captured items that were in storage, so we can assume the men would have presented a fairly motley appearance.

As for the Cairo National Guard formed from Europeans, if it ever existed, we can only assume its men wore their own civilian dress with a tricolour cockade.

# 6

# Conclusion, Sources, and Further Reading

As stated in the introduction to this book, it can have no real conclusion as it is research in progress. My deep desire is that it will prove first and foremost useful to enthusiasts, especially war-gamers, providing them with the hard-to-find facts that they typically look for. Secondly, I hope it will serve as an inspiration for other researchers who will dig up new sources. Thirdly, I hope it will invite the casual amateur to read more about the expedition to Egypt. For all of these, the following lines will hopefully provide some information.

The one obvious big challenge is the availability of information in the English language.

As regards general histories of the campaign, I would encourage the English-speaking reader to consult the following:

Christopher Herold's *Bonaparte in Egypt*: although this is an 'old' book, having first been published in the 1960s, it remains the best account in any language of Bonaparte's part of the expedition. Witty and highly readable it is the work of a historian who was born a Czech, spoke and wrote fluent English, and did this in the United States. He obviously had no nationalistic axe to grind and brings a neutrality to his account which is seriously lacking in similar French accounts. The book remains widely available, even in digital format.

Piers Mackesy's *British Victory in Egypt*: This is a much more recent volume, published in 1995. It is for me a model in military story-telling. Once again, a joy to read and packed with hard-to-find information. It relies heavily of course on Wilson's, Walsh's, and Reynier's accounts, but also draws on British archival material. It is also of prime importance for any Napoleonic enthusiasts as it readily explains how Abercromby's army actually formed the cradle of the future Peninsular leadership.

Juan Cole's 2007 *Napoleon's Egypt – Invading the Middle East* is the most recent account in the English language and draws an interesting and accurate comparison with recent events. However it stops at December 1798 and is thus not even as exhaustive as Herold's work.

There seems to be no detailed account in English of Kleber's campaign of Heliopolis.

# CONCLUSION, SOURCES, AND FURTHER READING

In this age of internet, many excellent primary accounts of the campaigns can be found:

Reynier's *State of Egypt after the Battle of Heliopolis* published in London in 1802 is a must-read to understand the context and climate within French leadership prior and during the British invasion. Napoleon never fully forgave Reynier for this harsh pamphlet against Menou.

Sir Robert Wilson's *History of the British expedition to Egypt* is a fundamental text from the British side and highly readable as is all of Wilson's prose. Walsh's *Journal of the Late Campaign in Egypt* is a junior officer's interesting view of the events.

On other aspects of the expedition and its consequences:

Carmel Testa's *The French in Malta 1798-1800* is a massive and definitive volume on this little-known topic. I have not gone into details concerning Vaubois' division and their stay in Malta in this book as its aim was squarely Egypt, but readers are strongly advised to consult this remarkable work done by a major Maltese historian.

Brian Lavery's *Nelson and the Nile, the Naval War against Bonaparte*, published in 1998 for the bicentennial of the victory pretty much covers it in great length and detail.

Stanford J. Shaw's *Between Old and New: The Ottoman Empire under Sultan Selim III 1789-1807* brushes the broader context of the Ottoman Empire and is interesting to consult.

Ian Coller's *Arab France 1798-1831* published in 2001 does not directly discuss the Egyptian campaign but more its aftermath and consequences on the first penetration of Arab culture in France

As regards memoirs, a few French memoirs have been translated, notably Jean-Pierre Doguereau: *Guns in the Desert. Journal of Napoleon's Egyptian Expedition*, and

Joseph-Marie Moiret: *Memoirs of Napoleon's Egyptian Expedition*. A key primary source is of course *Copies of Original Letters from the Army of General Bonaparte in Egypt*, published in 1798 and consisting of correspondence that had fallen into British hands. This is easily available on line and must be consulted as these are letters written at the time with no later wish to embellish the stories they tell.

Parts of other French memoirs and letters can be found in Herold's or Cole's volume (Cole especially refers to Bernoyer whose letters were not available to Herold at his time).

A must read is Al Jabarti's *History of Egypt*, of which several translations seem to have been made and which can be found in paperback or hardback versions. We unfortunately have very little Egyptian by way of primary sources and this is one which does paint a sometimes ironic image of the French in Egypt and vividly shows the cultural gap between West and East.

On the topic of uniforms, aside from the various volumes published by Osprey more or less directly related to the campaign, Charles Grant published two volumes of *Napoleon's Campaign in Egypt* with illustrations by Bob Marrion who had participated actively in one of the best studies on the topic done in France in the very early 1960s.

Obviously for those who read French, the list is far greater.

In terms of general histories, there is Henry Laurens' *Histoire de l'Expédition d'Égypte* which was published 1998 and is available in paperback. It is a good general overview but will leave short those with a taste for the military.

The one major reference remains the *Histoire Scientifique et Militaire de l'Expédition d'Égypte*. This massive multi-volume work was published in the 1830s by veterans of the expedition and drew considerably on primary notes, memoirs, etc. It also includes many of Dutertre's portraits. It is still to this day, probably the most comprehensive account of the overall expedition. It can be found online.

At the end of the 19th century, the new historical section of the French general staff, created after the defeat of 1870-1871, was tasked with publishing detailed accounts of the various campaigns of the past centuries. A senior officer, Clément de la Jonquière, set about this task for the Egyptian campaign. Unfortunately, he died before being able to complete it and then the First World War interrupted any further work on this. Still, de La Jonquière's exemplary work outlines almost day-by-day the expedition right up to Bonaparte's departure. He quotes almost entirely from the archives. It is the best possible way for anyone to have a first contact with the primary sources available in French archives. This work was wonderfully reprinted by bookseller Teissedre in 1998 and still available. He added a sixth volume which includes several other studies which complete to some degree the history beyond the summer of 1799.

Of note are two small booklets by Fabrice Delaître published by the small publishing company Historic'One in 2010 and 2011 in a series devoted to forgotten French battles: one is on Acre and Mount-Thabor, the other one is on Heliopolis and is the only volume focused on this battle.

Memoirs abound and many are available on line. More remarkably, an exhaustive bibliography of all memoirs related to Egypt (including in languages other than French) was published in 1993. The author, Philippe de Meulenaere, has taken the time to not only list them but also provides an analysis of each. This *Bibliographie Raisonnée des Témoignages de l'Expédition d'Égypte* is a must-have for anyone wishing to study this topic.

There have been numerous studies on specific topics ranging from sanitary conditions to the printing press. The topic of relationship between the French and the Egyptians, however, was only fairly recently addressed in detail. André Raymond's 2004 volume on *Égyptiens et Français au Caire 1798-1801* published by the French Institute of Oriental Archaeology (IFAO) draws heavily on local sources (especially tribunals) and although not an easy read is a refreshing view on the period.

Aside of the various histories and memoirs are the correspondences of the three key players. Bonaparte's correspondence was first published under Napoleon III. The volume related to Egypt can be found on line. However the second volume of the new edition of Napoleon's correspondence by Fayard (2005) is a much preferred volume as it is far more exhaustive and contains a wealth of additional information (organisation, relative currency values, etc.).

# CONCLUSION, SOURCES, AND FURTHER READING

Kléber's even more remarkable letters and notes were published by the IFAO in the 1990s. This comprehensive series in four volumes edited by Henry Laurens is another essential source for anyone wishing to understand the evolution of the army and Kleber's remarkable psyche.

There is no publication of Menou's letters other than in *Kléber et Menou en Égypte Depuis le Départ de Bonaparte*, available on line, which includes quite a selection of both generals' letters.

Finally we come to the B6 series of archives. In the early 19th century, all papers were considered as owned by the officer having them. Formal inclusion in public archives was not systematic and it is therefore amazing so much of the Army of the Orient papers have still managed to land in the French war archives. The correspondence registers of the three generals-in-chief and those of their chiefs of staff are of course essential. The archives also hold many of Daure's papers as they were bequeathed to the French archives. His correspondence registers organised by topics need to be carefully examined. His individual correspondence is however spread out throughout the correspondence boxes (over eighty!). The author has to confess he has not gone through all of them yet. Cavalier, former head of the Dromedaries, left to the archives his orderly books as well as an organisation register. These have been well used by many artists to come up with their rendering of the Dromedaries.

One important source which has not been compiled yet is the full set of the Army of Orient daily orders. These have been spread through several registers, some printed, some manuscript. The author has started undertaking their systematic transcription, as they provide a unique view of the life of the army in many aspects. Much of the anecdotes and information featured in this book have come from them. Hopefully this work will be finished in the next few years.

On uniforms the entire series of articles done by Albert Rigondaud in "Uniformes", then "Traditions" and lastly "Figurines" are the most exhaustive and most recent source. One can easily look at Rousselot's remarkable plates on-line via the French national museums photographic web site: www.photo.rmn.fr

The most comprehensive study on all armies was published privately in the 1960s by Jacques Brouillet, a well-known collector of the Orleans area. This series of plates covering French, British, and Turkish armies occasionally comes up for sale at auctions. Some of Brouillet's own studies on the British are visible on line as part of the Anne S.K. Brown military collection.

Henry Boisselier did several excellent studies on Egypt, however none were published. Again some watercolours by him show up and are worth checking out.

Finally, such an incredible adventure should have motivated many film makers. Actually, only one true film was ever made on the expedition. "Adieu Bonaparte" (Farewell Bonaparte) in 1984 by Egyptian film-maker Yussef Chahin. A rather big-budget picture in those days, it features some major French comedians in the main roles. However, the scenario and acting are now very dated, reflecting more the international politics of the 1980s than those of the late 1790s! Happily there have been a few documentaries which are much better: "Napoleon's Lost Fleet" (National Geographic) is a remarkable piece of underwater archaeology recounting the Battle of the Nile and what remnants one can still find in Aboukir Bay. The best documentary on the entire expedition is actually very recent as it was produced by the French-German TV channel ARTE in 2016 and broadcasted in the spring of 2017. Using 3D imaging, good actors and rather convincing costumes, this two-part feature manages to accurately cover both the military and scientific parts of the expedition in three hours. At the time of writing it is said that it will become available for the English-speaking world.

It is now time for me to conclude for now this work. I do know, by experience, that there is more to find and this conclusion is but temporary, as always with the Army of the Orient.